The Ultimate Travel Guide to Iceland for 2023, 2024, and Beyond

A Guidebook to this Beautiful Country –
Explore Reykjavík, Glaciers, Amazing Waterfalls,
the Northern Lights, and more

Andrew Hitchens

© **Copyright 2022 - All rights reserved.**

The content contained within this book may not be reproduced, duplicated or transmitted without direct written permission from the author or the publisher.

Under no circumstances will any blame or legal responsibility be held against the publisher, or author, for any damages, reparation, or monetary loss due to the information contained within this book, either directly or indirectly.

Legal Notice:

This book is copyright protected. It is only for personal use. You cannot amend, distribute, sell, use, quote or paraphrase any part, or the content within this book, without the consent of the author or publisher.

Disclaimer Notice:

Please note the information contained within this document is for educational and entertainment purposes only. All effort has been executed to present accurate, up to date, reliable, complete information. No warranties of any kind are declared or implied. Readers acknowledge that the author is not engaging in the rendering of legal, financial, medical or professional advice. The content within this book has been derived from various sources. Please consult a licensed professional before attempting any techniques outlined in this book.

By reading this document, the reader agrees that under no circumstances is the author responsible for any losses, direct or indirect, that are incurred as a result of the use of information contained within this document, including, but not limited to, errors, omissions, or inaccuracies.

Table of Contents

Reykjavík 6

Hafnarfjörður 20

Húsavík 26

Egilsstaðir 34

Vík í Mýrdal 38

Kópavogur 46

For the Perfect Picture 52

The Northern Lights 62

Less Visited Attractions that Deserve a Day Trip 68

If You Only Have One Week: (Sites, Camping, Hiking, Northern Lights) 72

Where to Eat in Iceland 76

Interesting & Traditional Foods 83

Icelandic Culture: What You Need to Know 90

Unique Holidays & Events 92

Visa Information 98

Tours & Cruises 99

Getting Around 104

Interesting Facts 110

References 113

Seljalandsfoss Waterfall

Population: 366,425 (2022)

Religion: 80% Lutheran Church, **5%** Practice Ásatrú (Norse/Viking Religion)

Currency: Icelandic Krona

Language Spoken: Icelandic (Official) **English** (Spoken by 95% of the population)

The country of Iceland has a unique and fascinating history that dates back to the age of the Vikings, where Norsemen first settled on the land of "Fire and Ice." Its history began with members of the British Isles and Norway being taken by Vikings and made to live in Newfoundland. The land of Iceland stood out to the Vikings as it was during their arrival time in the 800s that the climate was warm and full of natural resources to use. Today, there is still living evidence to look back on as proof of the group's lasting impact on this glorious land.

Iceland is one of the most beautiful countries in the entire world. Since its official date as a member of the EEA (European Economic Area), it has continuously ranked in top positions throughout the world. Iceland has been placed as the tenth best country out of a total of 198 contenders.

The Best Time of Year to Visit

1. <u>Summer (June, July, August):</u> The summer months are undoubtedly the best time of the year to travel to and throughout Iceland due to the lesser number of tourists. It may be surprising to know that these months are not the most popular time to visit. A reason for this may be that many people wish to experience the winter wonderland that Iceland is well known for. However, during June, July, and August, the weather is by far the warmest that it will be during any other season in the country. If you are wanting to see Iceland for a lower travel cost and fewer crowds, summer is

your best chance. This doesn't necessarily guarantee that harsh winds and random rainstorms will not occur, but the majority of the season sees calm and sunny days.

2. <u>Winter (December, January, February)</u>: The winter months may seem like a daunting time to travel to Iceland due to the already cold weather being highly illustrated in the winter, but it is actually one of the best. For one, winter is when the Northern Lights are highly visible and there are tons of amazing winter-themed activities to partake in. No matter what your plans are, it is essential that you pack warmly. These months are the coldest and require at least *one* waterproof jacket and boots. But no matter the harsh weather, the winter months aren't as cold as you might imagine given how close the country is to the North Pole. Iceland has been made into a popular spot for celebrating holidays and ensuring that one experiences a winter wonderland sensation that can most definitely be achieved while enjoying the warmth of the Blue Lagoon on a cold snowy day.

3. <u>Fall (September, October, November)</u>: The fall season is as good of a time as any to visit Iceland. These months typically see fewer crowds than the winter and spring months and often have limited days of harsh weather patterns. This is the best time to see the color changes from greens to

yellows and oranges. If your sole purpose for coming to Iceland is to see the wondrous Northern Lights, then these months may be your best chance at achieving this. September kicks off the first appearance of the year for the lights. Iceland's true fall months are generally categorized as being between the months of September and October but can lead into the month of November.

4. <u>Spring (March, April, May):</u> The spring months bring the most unpredictability to the weather in most of Iceland. It is also the time of year that gives the best chances at seeing the Northern Lights and avoiding snowstorms that clog roads and make it difficult to see some of the popular attractions such as the Golden Circle. The spring months are the perfect time of year to see Iceland's furry friends: puffins. Puffins make their way to the seaside cliffs and become active in the early evenings of the day. The spring also has something that beats the winter months and that is the lasting sunlight that hits it, making it worthy of a fun trip.

Reykjavík City Card: This city card holds all the power when using public transportation to get around the city. It works similarly to a bus pass but allows for more freedom on where and when you travel to your destination.

Where to Visit

Iceland is considerable in size in terms of land and mass. With a relatively small size of human population and the majority of all citizens living in the capital city, the most well-visited areas of the country have almost certainly remained the same for decades. These towns and cities are as follows: the capital of Reykjavík, Hafnarfjörður, Húsavík, Egilsstaðir, Vík í Mýrdal, and Kópavogur.

Reykjavík

● • ● • ● • ● • ● • ● • ● • ●

When most people think of Iceland, they more than likely will envision the captivating city of Reykjavík. This could be due to the overwhelmingly beautiful and colorful buildings, the close proximity to the Blue Lagoon and other attractions, or the fact that it is the capital. Whatever your reason for picturing the city or wanting to visit it, you can be sure that it remains one of the most well-traveled places in all of Iceland.

History:

Reykjavík has changed tremendously since it was officially founded in 1786 and given municipal powers by the Danish government. The city was once a port town that was used for the purpose of fishing and markets that brought in money and created stable living conditions for the small population. It wasn't until the 1700s that the population grew and the need for a larger administrative system was needed. But what seems to be a simple history is actually far more complex when discussing the past of Reykjavík.

Northman settler Ingólfur Arnarson was considered to be the first founder and discoverer of Reykjavík in the year 874 A.D. After he, his wife, and brother journeyed to find a new place to call their home after a blood feud forced him out of his town. Stories told over the centuries of Ingólfur's settlement have remained the same as the belief that upon searching for land at sea, Ingólfur threw large pillars into the water. He ensured everyone that he would create a land based on where the pillars would wash ashore. It was then that Reykjavík, named for the steam of the hot springs, was born.

Researchers are not entirely certain of Reykjavík's true founder as some evidence does point to Vikings being the first to set foot on the land. However, most of Iceland does recognize Ingólfur Arnarson to be the man responsible for creating their city.

Reykjavík's wealth has only increased throughout the years, especially during the Postwar Era. This time was a large turning point for the city as Iceland's neutrality in the wars brought allies that needed the help of the community to provide stable resources. Many citizens from rural parts of the country began moving to the larger and more populated city to sell large portions of locally caught fish. Not only did this stabilize the economy but also help to skyrocket it and put Reykjavík on the map for being a wealthy and reliable place to live. For this reason, Reykjavík holds the largest population of any other community in Iceland.

Where to Stay:

If you're on a budget: Loft - HI Hostel & Bar
https://www.hostel.is/Reykjavík

> » This hostel is perfect for travelers in need of a budget stay. Large room with air conditioning, within walking distance of major tourist sites, and lots of fun activities to partake in such as a game room and indoor bar.
> » If you're looking for luxury: The Retreat at Blue Lagoon Iceland
> https://www.bluelagoon.com/accommodation/retreat-hotel
> » It doesn't get more luxurious than accommodation situated directly on the Blue Lagoon. This hotel is more than just a place to stay. It is full of top-notch amenities and full and private access to the geothermal spa.
> » If you want fun: Eric the Red Guesthouse
> https://sites.google.com/view/eric-the-red-guesthouse/
> » The goldilocks for people looking for something between a hostel and a hotel. This accommodation offers the privacy and comfort of a hotel while also creating a sense of community with frequent long-stay travelers.

If you want unique: Reykjavík Domes
http://www.Reykjavíkdomes.com/

> » The Domes of Reykjavík offer a new way of seeing the city. Located just 10 minutes from the downtown area, these cozy "homes" give guests the chance to disconnect from the hustle and bustle of the city and instead surround themselves with the outdoors.

What to See & Do:

> » **Hallgrímskirkja**
>> o Among some of the tallest structures in the whole world is the Lutheran-based church of Hallgrímskirkja. The church took over forty years to complete after its commission in the 1940s. It has since become an icon for Icelandic architecture and is a must-see attraction. It is also likely the first thing that will catch your eye as soon as you take that step into Reykjavík. The people of Iceland are proud of this world-class structure that has a unique shape and history to it. It is most definitely important to get a few dozen photos or so in front of the Hallgrímskirkja.

- **Harpa**
  - Harpa is the home of Iceland's great symphony Orchestra that has worked as the main concert hall for performers for over a decade. The hall's architecture was designed to exhibit the image of Iceland's diverse and ever-changing landscape. It is why the head architect of the project, Henning Larsen, worked with local architects to get a feel for the Danish-Icelandic design that commissioners were looking for. Harpa's initial purpose has evolved over the years as it was first meant to be the beginning stage for what Iceland officials called "the World Trade Center Reykjavík." The World Trade Center would be a place for individuals to get together and enjoy shops, restaurants, music, and even apartments so people could live in the heart of all the action. However, Harpa's plans were put on hold during the 2008 financial crisis, and many wondered what would become of the ambitious site. What few could predict was just how inspirational citizens would find Harpa to be after it was eventually opened in 2011 and just how impactful it would be on Iceland's glowing reputation. Harpa is open to the general

public every day so even if you're not able to make a showing of one of the outstanding performances, you can still get a look inside this fabulous center.

» **Viðey Island**
  o One of Iceland's many islands is Viðey Island which is only accessible by ferry. This island can make for a day trip from Reykjavík as it is easy to get to from the capital city, especially in the summer months when the ferry runs more continuously. Visiting Viðey is a much different experience than other places in Iceland and is sure to make for a unique and exciting day. Artist Yoko Ono is partially responsible for putting this little island on the map and that is because of the commissioned work she did titled the Imagine Peace Tower. Ono's work was created as a way to represent her late husband, famed singer-songwriter John Lennon. The artwork is made up of an enormously tall array of lights as they are depicted against a stone monument. The words "Imagine Peace" are then displayed in over twenty different languages. Ono has continued to frequently visit Viðey and is a prominent supporter of the island's tourism

industry. Special occasions such as John Lennon's birthday and the anniversary of his death bring about the most visitors whether that be people from other parts of Iceland or simply from out of the country, these dates hold a special meaning for the island of Viðey. Outside of this special memorial is a wonderful place to discover art and culture. Museums, galleries, and the Viðeyjarstofa which showcases paintings from famous Icelandic artists are all within reach in Viðey. The best part is that most of these are free with the Reykjavík City Card!

» **Food Tour**
  - There are lots of ways to get used to a new city, country, or area. Walking around gets you a sense of the landscape, going to the tourist attractions lets you see what the country is famous for, and a traditional guide tells you some interesting facts about the area. A food tour, however, is one of the best ways to combine all of these things into one amazing event that gives you a sense of the most important thing: the culture. Getting to immerse into a new culture is a challenging endeavor, especially when on a strict time schedule. Going on a food

tour is an amazing way to see how a different region of the world from your own prepares, eats, and portrays its food. Food tours also often work simultaneously as a walking tour because the guide takes their guests throughout both popular and lesser traveled neighborhoods to get to the food stops. These types of tours are all for a look and feel for parts of the city that don't get as many visitors throughout the tourist months. The highlights of taking a food tour are also the connections that are made with the locals that run the restaurants, bakeries, cafes, and street food vendors. If you are wanting to leave your trip to Iceland knowing that you learned a lesson in Icelandic cooking, then a food tour is a must. They are also cost-efficient and easy to find in the city.

- **Elf School**
  - Going to Elf School is a pretty big accomplishment. For people that have a few extra days to spend in Iceland or simply are wanting something to do that is a bit unconventional, the Elf School is the perfect pit stop to make. As a student at school, you will learn all there is to know and more about elf culture, history,

folklore, mythical beings, Icelandic stories, and tons more. Students will gain a new perspective on what it means to be an elf in Iceland and all of the hidden spots that the creatures like to hide in all across Reykjavík. What more is that the Elf School often brings in special guest speakers to recount their own personal stories about their encounters with the elves themselves. After getting a good introduction to the lessons, everyone is welcome to a complimentary breakfast/lunch for the group(s) excited about all things elves. A walking tour guide is given to all of the students that participate in the classroom that takes everyone to some of the most popular hiding spots for the elves in the city. Folktales are told and illustrated with books, pictures, maps, and overall stories. These stories dive deep into the history of the creatures and their mythical relatives as they date back to the early years of Iceland. The Elf School is open all year round in Reykjavík, every Friday. The school itself takes 2–5 hours to complete, after which you and everyone else in the classroom will become certified elf experts. That's something fun to put on your resume!

- » **City Walk**
    - ○ Taking a walk is the best way to see all of the sites and enjoy Reykjavík. A city walk can be done through a walking tour group or simply alone as the city is an excellent place for people who love to get out and walk. There is no other way to truly see a city than to immerse yourself in the action. The best part about this activity on your list of things to do is that it's free and easy. Reykjavík is also designed to be a pedestrian-friendly city with attractions being close to one another and sidewalks on every corner. If you are on a budget, limited time, or simply want to make the most out of your journey to Iceland, take a city walk. Walking tours are usually done with a guide that is highly familiar with the area. While these are not always free, they are never too costly. They can be perfect for solo travelers that are wishing to meet like-minded travelers as well. Walking tours also tend to include lunch/dinner and even game nights after the walk.

- **"Free" Museums and Parks**
  - It is hard to find activities to partake in that don't cost at least $5 USD while in Iceland. For fans of museums, Iceland's are free for all guests (sort of). While some museums do charge an average cost of $14.50 for adults, there are some that waive this fee. On top of that, the majority of these museums that do cost a fee are not high in price and will often admit people aged eighteen or younger without any sort of payment. This means that you can easily spend an entire day of fun without having to spend too much money on them. If you can't get into the strolling and touring mood of going to a museum, then maybe consider spending an afternoon and/or evening at one of the many public parks. Iceland is home to a large range of relaxing and calming parks that anyone can visit. Some of these are actually national parks and are therefore not the typical image one may have when picturing walking through a public area. However, while it may take a bit more strategic planning, national parks are just as welcoming and even more beautiful to see than some of the public ones.

- **Fly Over Iceland**
  - Iceland receives many tourists and other travelers from all over the world throughout every season. This is mostly because of the breathtaking scenery that no other country seems to be able to fully capture the attention of an entire world the way that Iceland does. For many visitors, it can be intimidating to try and create an itinerary that allows for those traveling to the country to experience without at least multiple weeks to a month of staying to see all that there is to see. What better way to conquer this challenge than by flying over the island itself? There are many helicopters and small plane tours that anyone can take that give a full eye view of the nation and its beautiful land. These can range from short tours that last an hour to two, or they can be long tours with a more descriptive list of all that drives visitors to Iceland. Helicopter and plane tours can be reserved for small to large groups, one on one, or solo tours that work for anyone's needs.

- » **E-bike Through Town**
  - Like most big cities in Europe, Reykjavík has some amazing bike rental services that are low-cost and located all across the city. These are used not only by visitors but also by the locals as well. If you're worried about standing out as a tourist, these bikes won't make that happen. The city, while small, was built to be spread out. With E-bikes, the hassle of a car rental is gone and made easier with the easy access of these many bikes scattered across the city. Tours are given through the usage of these E-bikes and make for a fun day riding to the hidden gems of Reykjavík.

- » **Icelandic Punk Museum**
  - A tiny museum that packs one hell of a punch: The Punk Museum! For those unaware, the idea of Reykjavík being a staple destination in the punk community may come as a shock given its more laid-back, small-town charm. Surprisingly, the 1970s through 1990s saw a huge wave of punk music and the self-identified "punker," aka those who found a community among people with similar music taste to themselves. At this museum, you will find records, photos,

posters, leather jackets, toilets used as art, and much much more. Even more interesting, this destination was once used as an underground restroom for the city center of Reykjavík. If your love for the 70s–90s punk museums never went away, then be sure to make a pit stop at the Icelandic Punk Museum. (Admission: 1000–1200 Icelandic krona)

Hafnarfjörður

● • ● • ● • ● • ● • ● • ●

Where to Stay:

If you're on a budget: Lava Hostel https://lavahostel.is/

» The Lava Hostel is a laid-back, budget-friendly option for travelers that are seeking the easy convenience of short drives to popular destinations. The hostel offers both private and shared dorm-style rooms as well as a camping option that is right outside of the housing quarters. Close to both the international airport and the city buses, you can't go wrong with staying at this accommodation while in Hafnarfjörður.

If you're looking for luxury: Design Cottage Close to Icelandic Countryside & Reykjavík
https://www.airbnb.co.uk/rooms/plus/18736637?adults=1&children=0&infants=0&check_in=2023-03-27&check_out=2023-04-03&federated_search_id=1011d5d2-60a9-4914-ae18-

5d25e3716fde&source_impression_id=p3_1660660717_EQtztbdjYmhxbi0L

- » This is the perfect cottage for getting to know the area. This home focuses on giving its guests a cozy feeling of being one with nature while providing a gorgeous patio for guests to relax at. Staying here, you may take note of the California feel to it as the owners of this home have utilized their past travels to the state as inspiration for the design elements used throughout this Airbnb. For only 166 euros a night, this cottage provides a luxurious amount of amenities and goods at an affordable price while also remaining located in close proximity to the main city center.

If you want fun: Hotel Viking
https://www.hotelviking.com/?utm_source=google-gbp&utm_medium=organic&utm_campaign=gbp

- » Hotel Viking is the type of hotel that you never want to have to leave. Inspired by Nordic culture, each hotel room takes a piece of this Nordic history as inspiration for creating a themed base environment. Here you can enjoy a Viking-prepared meal and a luxurious sauna room all for free.

If you want unique: Adorable 1-bedroom guesthouse in Hafnarfjörður
https://www.airbnb.co.uk/rooms/578056205602364614?adults=1&children=0&infants=0&check_in=2023-02-05&check_out=2023-02-12&federated_search_id=1011d5d2-60a9-4914-ae18-5d25e3716fde&source_impression_id=p3_1660660762_ABb0c%2FHWgvjLAC5N

» This private guesthouse has everything that one could need for their travels to Hafnarfjörður. Just a ten-minute drive from Reykjavík and twenty minutes from the airport, this home features elegant rooms and a garden view.

What to See & Do:

» **Explore Hafnarfjörður**
  o Sometimes referred to as the 'Town in the Lava' or 'Town of the Elves,' the town of Hafnarfjörður has all the joys of being in close proximity to Reykjavík but with the same town feel of a traditional community in Iceland.
  o The town has a fabulous museum that features art from around the country as well as local artists that have made a profound impact on the cultural history of Hafnarfjörður.

- » **The Viking Village and Viking Festival**
  - ○ The most well-known thing about Iceland is its close history to the Vikings that once pirated their way through the country during the 870s A.D. The town of Hafnarfjörður has been given the nickname of the Town of Elves due to its large history of Viking stories and love for the culture. It is such an important aspect of the town that every year a fun and interactive Viking festival occurs. The annual event includes participants dressing up in traditional Viking clothing, cooking a Viking meal, and participants playing games that include ax throwing and crossbow. There is even an exclusive Viking club that members of the town can try and get into to show their support for the Viking culture in their town.
- » **Thingvellir Hiking**
  - ○ There are lots of places to go hiking in Iceland that ensure perfect conditions for all levels of hiking experience. The Thingvellir hiking trail is one of these that is fit for most hikers with little to no experience. The majority of the trail is paved and flat, meaning there is a simplicity to the terrain. It is also beautiful with views of the mountains, streams, and trees all around. It makes for a nice walk for photographers as well, given the many small white painted churches and

other buildings that line the area. The many farms and wildlife that one can spot while hiking this trail are endless and make for a nice day spent in nature.

» **Thríhnúkagígur Volcano**
  o Discovered in 1974 by explorer Árni B. Stefánsson, the Thríhnúkagígur volcano is one of the most easily accessible volcanoes for explorers to venture into. This is because it has been reported that the last time it erupted was nearly 4,000 years ago! This is an incredible claim because of the fact that it is both taller than the Statue of Liberty and has a ground floor space of 160x220 feet, meaning it is absolutely huge. Taking a tour of this site is an out-of-this-world experience that lasts for 5–6 hours with participants being able to actually go inside the volcano. Guests are descended 400 feet below ground and given the chance to hike through the space for a total of 2 miles across the space. Tours are available during specific times of the seasons and change yearly. Check the official website for more information. <https://insidethevolcano.com/>

» **Leiðarendi Lava Cave**
  o Located in the Blue Mountain, the Lava Cave tour is an encouraged activity for people that have an interest in mysteries, folklore, and magic. Many citizens of

Iceland believe that this cave is one of the many homes of the trolls that are thought to live in the country. It is also thought to be the resting place of ghosts that previously died inside the cave itself. This is because during cold winters, many citizens without homes would make a basecamp inside the space in an attempt to stay warm. Unfortunately, this did not always ensure comfort, and during the Great Depression, there was a large influx of Icelanders who lost their lives inside Lava Cave. But while this space does have a dark history to it, it is a part of Iceland's history that makes it so unique to visit. The Lava Cave is also without a doubt stunning to see. It is covered in bright oranges and reds that depict the color of lava (hence the name) and is covered in hanging icicles throughout the colder months. With a tour and guide, the Leiðarendi Lava Cave is worth checking out.

HÚSAVÍK

• • • • • • • • • • • • •

Where to Stay:

If you're on a budget: Húsavík Cape Hotel
https://www.Húsavíkhotel.com/

» This family-run hotel is described by its owners as being a combination of an accommodation and a museum. The interior is decorated with past explorers' expeditions and relics. It has also been the place where artists have come to sell their work and donate artifacts that have been found throughout the country of Iceland. If you are a big history lover or someone that wants to truly immerse themselves in some of Iceland's great past, then staying at the Húsavík Cape Hotel is the place to book your travels to and enjoy them on a budget.

If you're looking for luxury: Fosshotel Húsavík
https://www.islandshotel.is/hotels-in-iceland/fosshotel-Húsavík

> » The Fosshotel has the best views of the town through every window of their rooms. It is the center hub for local attractions and the many whale-watching tours that come from out of Húsavík. These modern and stylish rooms come fully equipped with a mini fridge, flatscreen television, and the perks of their amazing bistro and bar. Fosshotel has been ranked the number one hotel and place to stay for conferences that occur throughout the entirety of Iceland. An added bonus for staying here is the tours and travel packages that are offered to guests for discounted prices and inside scoop deals that you cannot receive anywhere else.

If you want fun: Árból Guesthouse https://arbol.is/

> » Árból Guesthouse brings to life the family-owned business vibes that everyone searches for during their trip away from home. It is a cozy and well-respected accommodation that is situated right in the heart of downtown Húsavík. Fresh breakfast is served to guests every morning free of charge and guests are encouraged to branch out and talk to other travelers experiencing Iceland.

> » (Community-styled shared bathrooms)

If you want unique: Húsavík Green Hostel
https://www.Húsavíkgreenhostel.is/

> » If you are on a tight budget, then staying in a hostel is a great alternative to traditional-style hotels. Húsavík Green Hostel makes traveling to Iceland (one of the most expensive European countries) easy to do with limited funds. What's more is that Green Hostel is completely environmentally and eco-friendly. The feel of this hostel is quaint and farm-like with a wide range of outdoor activities to partake in without the need to spend money on tours and other events.

History:

The history of Húsavík stems from legends, mystery, and the bizarre intrigue that whales seem to have to it. Its uniqueness as a town has earned it the title of "Bay of the Houses." Húsavík has also been given the title of being the whale-watching capital of the world due to the many recorded number of whales that frequently visit the town every year. The amount of whales and whale species that spend their time in the waters of Húsavík have proven to be remarkable and have therefore earned the Whale Museum that visitors are encouraged to visit during their time in the town.

What to See & Do:

- **Go to the Whale Museum**
    - The Húsavík Whale Museum has made a name for itself as being a top non-profit organization that has worked hard to create a lasting exhibit that values the whale species. The museum houses eight consistent exhibitions as well as rotating events. These include the Whale Walk exhibition that showcases a number of whale skeletons, the Ocean of Plastics that tells the haunting story of how plastic is harming the open waters and how we as humans can help, and the Whaling History exhibition that promotes the geographical paths taken by whales on their way to Iceland every year. For visitors with children, the Whale School that is offered by the museum is a fun and interactive way to get first-hand knowledge about the local whales and their impact on the world. The museum also brings in a heavy amount of awareness about the whales of the world and how to protect them by throwing an annual Whale Congress meeting where researchers from all over the world can get together. There, experts discuss any new information found about the area,

the whales, and the environment as a whole. The museum is open all year round with opening and closing times changing depending on the season.

» **Walk around the Culture House**
- This attraction has remained on the list of the top ten things to do and see in Húsavík for the last five years. The museum/farm dates back to Iceland's first settlements. The farm and its houses function as a place for visitors to get a feel for what homes were like centuries ago. There are also multiple artifacts that are greatly a part of Iceland's history that can be seen at the Culture House.

» **Take a private tour with the Lava Horses**
- The Lava Horses tour takes you through the most scenic trails of all of Húsavík. Using trained horses, you will be sent alongside areas of wetlands, sandy terrain, forests, and of course lava. It is a top outdoor activity with trained, well-behaved horses and a trusted guide that is knowledgeable of the areas. Lava Horses tour is ideal for visitors that want the full nature experience while also remaining in a calm environment.

- **Go whale watching**
  - It goes without saying that whale watching is a popular sport for people to participate in when coming to Iceland. There is an abundance of whale-watching tours and groups that can be taken throughout the many small towns and cities in the country. Húsavík is just one of these places where whale watching remains the top attraction and is recommended to those not afraid of going out to sea. These exciting tours are amazing everywhere but there is something special about the way in which they are done in Húsavík. This may be because of the sheer number of whale species that like to arrive in the town unexpectedly. It also may be because of the Whale Museum that Húsavík has created that adds a special flare to these whale-watching tours as it shows the love and respect that locals have for the mammal. Whatever the case, if you are hesitant to spend the day on a boat filled with other curious minds of the many whales that have made Húsavík their home, take the leap and book a tour.

- **Geothermal baths**
    - Iceland has geothermal baths all over the country. It is why the Blue Lagoon is the most visited site for tourists to see, however, the town of Húsavík has the lesser known Geosea-Geothermal Sea Baths that is a world class experience. This natural heating seawater was discovered as somewhat of a happy accident when the land was drilled in an attempt to gain suitable water for houses. The water was instead too warm to be considered safe for the everyday use of the homes, however, with the help of local geniuses that did not want the water to be at a standstill, it was built into this wonderful resort. This unique seawater has since become famous for its proclaimed "miracle" working minerals that help with multiple skin issues and general pain relief.
- **A day at Puffin Island**
    - Puffin Island is exactly what it sounds like—an island filled with the adorable puffin animals. This uninhabited land is the home of the largest colony of puffins in the world. With the help of a guided tour that can be taken as a group or with a private company, you can see the place

where one-fifth of the world's puffin population lives and thrives.

Egilsstaðir

• • • • • • • • • • • • •

History: Iceland's large and cozy town was established in 1947 as Iceland began to expand into more rural parts of the country. The town has had a history that dates back to the 15th century as it was the home base for legislation to create and pass important acts and bills. It is the geography of the small community that has kept Egilsstaðir on the map for top places to visit in Iceland. As the total population is only around 3,000, the area has been able to remain a rural and eco-friendly place to live. It is also the only place in the entire country that you may be able to spot a reindeer out in the wild lands of rocky and snowy terrain.

Where to Stay:

If you're on a budget: Óbót 1. — riverside cabin
https://www.airbnb.com/rooms/

» This quaint Airbnb is perfect for travelers that want to be smack center in the outdoors and who have a love for fishing as the nearby river Rangá allows for free fishing! It is within a short drive to the airport and the Egilsstaðir countryside.

If you're looking for luxury: Downtown Egilsstaðir Apartment 1 https://www.airbnb.com/rooms/43567531?source_impression_id=p3_1662187721_t30CaRw6f%2FkLzgy4

» This is an entire rental unit home that acts as the perfect private getaway for visitors of the area. It is a large apartment with multiple beds that encourages long-term stays for people that want to add a couple extra nights to their stay in Egilsstaðir. Close to the downtown area with all of the amazing restaurants, bars, and local culture is what makes this such a great place to stay. A plus is that even with this accommodation getting the win for the luxury spot, it is still affordable at only 100 USD a night.

If you want fun: Adorable little guesthouse with private bathroom https://www.airbnb.com/rooms/5544249?

» Rent this entire charming cottage in the middle of the Egilsstaðir country fields. It is a tranquil and relaxing home that has all of the needed amenities for guests to enjoy. For rainy days, guests can sit out on the outdoor porch and embrace the nature surrounding the area.

If you want unique: Beautiful Cottage at Kaldá Lyngholt
<https://www.airbnb.com/>

» This small home is run on a family-owned farm just outside of the main city center of Egilsstaðir. The name of this cottage is perfect for its description as it really is a beautiful home that is surrounded by lush trees and forests as well as the Northern Lights. Provided for guests are clean linen towels, coffee/tea, and the usage of the calming hot tub located on the property. Get this incredible stay with a self check-in system for 239 USD a night.

What to See & Do:

» **Fardagafoss Waterfall hike**
  o This is a famous waterfall that photographers and hikers will love to encounter. The hike itself is not too challenging so long as the appropriate shoes and attire are planned. Once at the waterfall, it remains to be a favored excursion in the east region of Iceland.

» **The oasis of Stórurð**
  o Getting to Stórurð is no easy journey but the end result is some of the best views in the country to see. The hike officially begins at the Vatnskarð Service Center and is just the first step in a long journey

to discovering Iceland's number one gem. The conclusion of this hike is filled with snowy mountains, turquoise waters, and rocky landscapes.

» **Laugarfell hot springs**
  - These two natural hot springs overlook Mt. Snæfell in all its glory. It is said in old Folk tales that after a dip in these waters, magical healing powers begin to occur. You can even enjoy a night at the hot springs or rest for the day with a relaxing breakfast or dinner at the Laugarfell restaurant.

» **Ring Road Route 1 Road Trip**
  - A journey across the Ring Road Route 1 can take anywhere from six to twelve days depending on the season that your road trip is taking place in. This famous two-lane road is the only one of its kind as the route takes you through a circle across all of Iceland. It is the best way to see the country and its landscapes. This incredible road trip can first begin in Egilsstaðir and is recommended to last around fifteen days to ensure all major sites are seen and appreciated.

Vík í Mýrdal

• • • • • • • • • • • • •

When looking to book somewhere outside of the more well-known and visited area of Iceland, look no further than Vík. Vík was first recorded in history around the early 9th century and soon transformed into a major trading route. Vík became known as the main place to buy items that were deemed difficult to find such as flour, sugar, and types of fruit. The community of Vík grew increasingly large during the 1890s and early 1900s as Iceland's southernmost village began to garner more attention. The location of the town was perfect for new settlers looking to make a new home. Vík's enticing landscape made it an even more fascinating place to settle into as it is there that the widely known black sand beach is located. The town quickly put itself on the map when it comes to places to travel to. This is because of the insane natural beauty that lurks all around the town's edges. This includes volcanoes, beaches, waterfalls, lagoons, and hot springs. The amazing thing about Vík í Mýrdal is that even with the large amount of things to do and see, it has still remained to be a lesser traveled spot in Iceland, with it tending to lose to Reykjavík as the primary travel destination. Vík however, should not be missed. It is a place of wonders that anyone will enjoy and with such a long history, there are many historical relevant architectures and things to see.

Where to Stay:

If you're on a budget: Lovely 1-bedroom apartment close to Black Beach https://www.airbnb.com/rooms

» This one-bedroom, one-bathroom Airbnb is the perfect little oasis for travelers on a budget. Here you will find peace and quiet in a tranquil setting of the countryside and views of the sea. It is a nice change of pace to the bustling city of Reykjavík and is nearby multiple Vík attractions. This accommodation also has the added luxury of a balcony to enjoy a cup of coffee or tea during the mornings before your adventures. Even more helpful is the ability to have a self check-in system that allows for guests to make themselves at home as soon as they arrive at the host's home.

If you're looking for luxury: Hótel Vík
https://www.stayinvik.is/

> » This truly is a luxurious place to stay in Vík. This beautiful location is in the heart of Vík's scenic landscape. Created with modern finishes and a sleek design, this hotel is equipped for all your travel needs and wishes. For long-term stays, Hótel Vík provides cottages and apartments as alternatives to a traditional hotel room. These are stunning rooms and homes that come at an affordable price for the types of add-ons that are included. The Hótel Vík also comes with a restaurant and bar that is open every day of the week.

If you want fun: Hótel Kría https://www.hotelkria.is/

> » Hótel Kría is a type of accommodation that strives to make its guests feel comfortable and taken care of during their stay in Vík. This is why the hotel offers a variety of top-notch tours that can be taken by expert guides. There are over seventy tours that can be booked during your stay with no need to worry about transportation as a shuttle is provided. This is the perfect place to

stay if you are looking for convenience as there is daily breakfast, a first-class restaurant with classic Icelandic cuisine, and a nightly cocktail bar. What's more is that with the close proximity to the Northern Lights, you can literally go to sleep with the aurora borealis from your hotel bed.

If you want unique: Black Beach Suites
https://www.airbnb.com/rooms/

» Pictures and a simple description do not do this place justice. This is definitely one of the most unique stays in Vík. Located directly near the famous black sand beach and the home of the puffins, this suite-style apartment housing is an unbelievable stay. The home is designed to have a separation from the kitchen/living room to the bedroom, meaning that it feels airy and open for guests to walk around feeling relaxed. Nearby hiking is also a plus when booking at this Airbnb. For just 340 USD a night, you can stay at this incredible home.

What to See & Do:

» **Reynisfjara: Black Sand Beach**
  o Perhaps the area that truly puts Vík í Mýrdal on the map is its incredible beach that is covered in black sand. The beach has been ranked as one of the top ten

spots for non-tropical beaches in the whole world!

- An instantly recognizable place, Reynisfjara has been used for filming on the sets of television shows, Game of Thrones, Star Trek, and Vikings.
- It has also been the spot of many famous folklore stories that depict the tall standing basalt columns as being former trolls that were transformed as punishment.
- This area is the perfect spot for observing Iceland's natural and unique landscapes.

» **Katla Ice Cave Kerlingardalsvegur**
- *The best way to see this site is to go through a tour company due to the easy access that a tour guide will give you.*
- The Katla Ice Cave is on many people's bucket lists, and it is not difficult to see why. The first part of the journey to see the cave is by partaking in a relatively easy hike that takes only 10–15 minutes to complete. You will walk through streams, planks, and rocks to get to the destination. Once arrived, you will be able to witness the charcoal-colored cave walls

and the icy blue interior of the caves themselves.

- It is a most impressive experience when you discover that multiple volcanic eruptions created the caves and that Vikings from 800 A.D. were witnesses to these eruptions.

- A fitting end to the excursion allows for a shot of either Icelandic Brennivín schnapps on the rocks or simple water on the rocks.

» **The Friendship Statue**
- This sculpture that was unveiled in 2006 has a special history to it. It was commissioned to symbolize the sisterhood or friendship between Iceland and the UK. An almost identical one is found in the city of East Yorkshire, UK, and is a popular destination for people traveling to both destinations. It is a fun place to go with a friend, sibling, or significant other to represent the love that is shared.

- The Friendship Statue is often referred to by its tall appearance and leaning structure.

- **Reyniskirkja Church**
    - If you didn't know you were in Iceland, you would as soon as you stumbled upon the Reyniskirkja Church. This is due to its traditional Icelandic appearance of white wooden architecture, a pointed rooftop, and the obvious bright red contrast features.
    - Located atop a snowy mountain and luscious green grass, Reyniskirkja Church is the perfect spot for pictures and a quick day trip. It is important to note that the church is viewed as a sacred and important spot and is therefore only open and available to tourists during specific days and holidays.
- **Ziplining through Vík**
    - The town of Vík is a top spot for taking in the natural beauty of the country. Ziplining through it is a great way to take in all the sights, especially if time is a factor. Most tours run for 1.5–2 hours and take you through areas that feature waterfalls, rivers, and small villages. There is usually a small amount of hiking that is required to get to the zipline bases; however, these are not considered challenging and do allow for visitors to see more of the area of Vík.

- o For fans of history and culture, there is also a short lesson about the town and its neighboring villages.

» **Solheimajokull Glacier**
  - o One of Iceland's most accessible glaciers to hike to is Solheimajokull. This glacier was formed by two neighboring volcanic eruptions that are estimated to be some of Iceland's largest in history.

  - o Here you will find many ice caves and water running streams throughout the glaciers. Tours for this hike are not necessary but are encouraged as nearby waterfalls may be accessible as well by a tour guide. Certain areas require specific equipment that is best done with a professional tour and gives much more available to the beautiful Solheimajokull Glacier of Vík.

KÓPAVOGUR

● ● ● ● ● ● ● ● ● ● ● ● ●

History: Kópavogur has played an important role in the history of Iceland and therefore has some interesting facts itself. It is the largest town outside of Reykjavík neighboring communities and has a decent-sized population of over 40 thousand residents. Known by its nickname "Seal Pup Bay," Kópavogur is the home of many seals that have resided in the oldest parts of the town for years. The town has remained a part of a lasting history due to it being the site of the 1662 Kópavogur meeting. This was a memorable meeting as it was the one that finally gave Iceland the approval of joining Denmark-Norway. Historians will take this town in special interest as it remains a unique part of Iceland's diverse history and culture.

Where to Stay:

If you're on a budget: Hótel Ísland Comfort
https://uk.hotels.com/ho274182/hotel-smari-Kópavogur-iceland/

» This hotel comes with everything that you need during your stay in Kópavogur. What makes this a special place to stay is that it is close to Reykjavík airport and has a shuttle service to and from the hotel. The best thing that guests have to say about Hótel Ísland Comfort is that you get comfort, convenience, and helpful staff at a low cost. This hotel is an exceptional choice for travelers that wish to have a good stay with tasty food and a comfortable sleep.

If you're looking for luxury: 201 Hotel
https://uk.hotels.com/ho657707840/201-hotel-Kópavogur-iceland/

» A bit of a "fancy" hotel, the 201 Hotel is completely equipped with a fully stocked bar, gym, blackout curtains, and ticket/tour assistance. This hotel is made in a sleek style with modern finishes while being the perfect place for large groups or families. All couches can be used as beds, roll-out beds are available, and large double suites are also possible for booking. This location is next to a beautiful lake that is the home of multiple families of ducks that like to paddle around during the snowy winters and warm summers.

If you want fun: Hotel Kriunes - A city hotel by the lake
https://uk.hotels.com/ho443167/hotel-kriunes-a-city-hotel-by-the-lake-Kópavogur-iceland/

> » This hotel is fully equipped with a sauna, outdoor pool, spa tub, garden, and terrace. It is a stunning ranch-style accommodation that aims to bring nature right to your front door. It is located near where the Northern Lights frequently make an appearance and is designed to resemble a woodsy feel as guests can immerse themselves in the world of the outdoors. It is a very accommodating hotel and staff that has an incredible daily buffet and rental car/shuttle service.

If you want unique: Hótel Heiðmörk
https://uk.hotels.com/ho655550368/hotel-hei-mork-Kópavogur-iceland/

> » Getting a unique hotel in any part of Iceland that is not Reykjavík can be difficult. Most destinations outside of the major city in Iceland do not receive an influx of visitors to warrant an extravagantly unique accommodation. However, the Hótel Heiðmörk is a wonderfully fun stay for each of its guests. While there is a simplicity to this hotel, what makes it unique is the amount of care that workers put into making sure that

everyone is happy and getting what they need out of their stay.

What to See & Do:

» The town of Kópavogur is the second largest populated county in the country and sits just below the capital city of Reykjavík. The town is often used by tourists as a way to get cheaper accommodations and easy access to some of the popular destinations. For example, the Blue Lagoon. While Kópavogur is not the most recognized spot in Iceland to visit, it can be a fun place to stop by and see what a true Icelandic town looks and feels like.

- Horseback riding, swimming, and museum tours are available in Kópavogur for a fun day of activities.

» **Museum of Design and Applied Arts**
- Iceland's love and appreciation for the arts never ceases to impress. The Museum of Design and Applied Arts is just one of the many fabulous places to see the high level of creativity that artists from around Iceland, as well as other parts of the world, are capable of producing. This local museum truly packs a punch when it comes to showcasing inspiring works of art. For fans of graphic

design and the decades of the 60's, 70's, and 80's, this museum is for you. While most of the exhibits are on but one floor, the innovation that is present makes up for it being a relatively small museum.

» **Go hiking or walking**
   - A simple activity like hiking or walking is never boring in Kópavogur. The views are impeccable all year round making it just what the soul needs while visiting Iceland. Trails can differ in skill level from beginner to moderate to skilled. These each depend on altitude level, terrain (rocky and/or volcanic), or length and time of the trail to complete.

   - Recommendations:
     - Sandfell, Vifilfell, Inside the Volcano Trail, Blafjoll

» **Snowmobile Tour**
   - Going on a snowmobiling tour works for two ways. One—it is a fun and exciting activity that is an A+ for adrenaline junkies. Two—it can work as a way to see the sights as well. Taking a tour with a snowmobile will likely take you to all of the nearby glaciers and any small waterfalls.

- **Scientist Escape Room**
  - Escape rooms are a beloved game that can be taken in groups or as a solo participant. Luckily, there is a popular Scientist Escape Room located in the heart of the town.

For the Perfect Picture[1]

• • • • • • • • • • • • • •

There are many places in the world that are "picture-perfect," but going up against Iceland for this title is a hard challenge to win. With a country of hot springs, lava fields, black sand beaches, green valleys, and glistening lagoons, it is obvious why Iceland is the best place to get that Instagram-worthy photo shoot done—no filter needed.

» Hraunfossar: If you think that Hraunfossar is not worth the trip because it is "just a waterfall," then you would be very much mistaken. This *series* of waterfalls is one of Iceland's most famous natural creations that was formed as a result of a nearby volcanic eruption that was made by the Langjökull glacier. With the volcano's shared environment, the waterfalls have evolved into producing brightly colored orange, red, and

---

[1] Pixabay: Blue Lagoon Thermal Pool (Image)

yellow landscapes throughout its rocky terrain. Combined with the multiple twisty-shaped water flows, Hraunfossar is by far one of the best places in the country to achieve high-quality photos.

» 1973 US Navy C-117D Sólheimasandur Crash: This infamous crash site has become a go-to place for photographers visiting Iceland. There are quite a few reasons for this that tend to stem from the unique and inspiring history of the site. More recently it gained immense popularity when it was part of a music video shot for the musical Justin Bieber. The crash that is otherwise known as the DC3 plane crash cause was never properly announced but experts did later determine that the reason for the event was either a mistake made by one of the pilots involving the fuel tanks, or harsh weather patterns that had to do with ice formations on the wings. No matter the exact reason, the plane was never moved from its crash site and has since become a popular spot to get photos of the somewhat haunting beautiful image. The standout reason for this place is the random feature of the plane as its durability has faded throughout the years in contrast to the empty black sand beach that it sits on. Photographers enjoy this spot in Iceland because of its uniqueness but also because it is not often visited by the everyday type of tourist. While there may be crowds on certain days of the year, it is overall a spot to stop at to get some award-winning pictures.

» Seljalandsfoss: Located in the South Region of Iceland is the widely photographed Seljalandsfoss waterfall. This massive waterfall is accessible by a quick thirty-minute walk and is ranked to be a pretty easy walk to the top. There are too many things that make this waterfall so special and one of which is a somewhat hidden gem that has questionably gone unnoticed for years. The first amazing thing is that this is the most famous waterfall that people are actually able to go behind. It is for this reason that some astonishing photographers have published this view. The second unique thing is the Gljúfrabúi waterfall that is a mere 150 meters away from Seljalandsfoss. In contrast to its neighbor, Gljúfrabúi has far fewer visitors making it a great place to get away from the crowds. It is also slightly more difficult to find and is immersed in the nature of overgrown trees and branches. Both of these are amazing sights to see and make for an incredible adventure.

» Reykjanes Lighthouse: The Valahnúkur (or Reykjanes) Lighthouse was first constructed in 1878 as the one and only lighthouse in Valahnúkur. After seeing its fair share of natural disasters that brought damage and the possibility of demise, the city decided to rebuild the structure to be more stable and able to withstand unpredictable conditions. In 1908 the new lighthouse was built and completed. It was described as being completely marvelous and was, therefore, voted to be the best one in all of Iceland. Its incredible location is one of the reasons why this vote was achieved. Sitting on top of an empty field, the lighthouse has outstanding views of the land. In addition to that, the lighthouse is also within a short distance of the Blue Lagoon and other major areas to see in Iceland. If you want to snap some good pictures of the structure, then it is not hard to miss. The tall height on which it stands, the bright white color it's painted, and the vast open mountain that it was built on make for an easy-to-take photo.

» Brúarfoss: Iceland's bluest waterfall is a gorgeous place to take pictures of and at. In fact, the water comes from a nearby glacier and gives it its lively light blue and white color that is clear, cold, and striking. To get there a hike is required but the hike itself could be on this list of picture-perfect places to go to as it is just as breathtaking. The hiking route takes you through many other small waterfalls along the way that will eventually lead to the "big guy." The hike also goes through tiny streams and fences that may seem unconventional for a hike but actually make for some interesting and fun times that are a great treat for those seeking some adventure. Once at the Brúarfoss waterfall, the photos come easy. Surrounded by greenery and rocky terrain, the color of the water is the highlight feature of this hiking trip. Every which way you look, you will see the many starting points of the waterfall, as much of the area is covered in flowing water. Even with the somewhat out-of-the-way requirements that are a must for getting to the spot, it is more than worth it for the one-of-a-kind pictures that are the end result.

» Blue Lagoon: If you have any form of social media, then odds are you have come across a picture of someone in this Icelandic hot spring, covering their face in the white mud-like substance. As odd as it may sound, this is actually the main reason that the Blue Lagoon brings in so many visitors from so many countries and cities. This landmark has become an attraction so familiar as being from Iceland. It is one of the twenty-five wonders of the world and is a special place to visit since it is a man-made spa. People travel from all over the world to try out the geothermal waters for their skin benefits and relaxing remedies. A plus for visiting the Blue Lagoon is that no matter what time of the year it is or the weather that is hitting Iceland, the hot spring is open every day of the week so you can rest assured that that outstanding photo can be taken.

As Seen on TikTok

Social media has always played an important role in our lives, and this includes the world of travel and exploration. With so many posts and videos dedicated to adventure sports, it can be a good idea to look to the app TikTok for ideas of where to go and what to see. If you're wanting to find some unconventional travel plans to partake in or just want to know if something is worth seeing, here is a list of the top TikTok recommended locations:

» Midnight Sun: The summer months for countries that are near the Antarctic Circle get to experience a beautiful phenomenon called the Midnight Sun. Iceland is one of these lucky countries where this event occurs usually on June 21st of every year. While Iceland tends to be famous for its showing of the Northern Lights, the Midnight Sun is actually just as beautiful and awe-striking, if not more so given that there is such a short amount of time to witness it. Just one hour from Reykjavík is the Southern region of the country where it is the best location to see the sun appear at midnight. It is something that everyone wishes to capture on film and makes for one amazing video. This is why it should come as no surprise that the community of travelers on TikTok has found a love for the Midnight Sun.

» Basaltic Prisms (Stuðlagil Canyon): Iceland's natural wonders never cease to amaze, but these basaltic prisms are probably one of the most recorded on TikTok. When you see them, it all makes sense as to why the canyon of these prisms has taken over the social media platform. The basaltic prisms are formed from all sorts of shapes and sizes that are seen in contrast with the turquoise-colored stream water with green mountains in the background. What's most interesting about this spot is just how long this wonderland went without ever receiving a visitor. It was only around 2018 that these prisms began to get the type of recognition that it deserved. Going now, more than likely you will encounter a bit of a crowd, but a crowd in Iceland is necessarily what you'd expect. Since there are so many amazing places to visit in the country, the canyon hardly ever encounters a major storm of people arriving throughout the year. It is definitely a place to go to be one with nature and to relax to the sound of the water rushing past. To get there, a hike is required. Depending on where you are entering from, certain areas may be closed off due to rising water levels. Luckily, there are guides to help you along with your journey as well as locals that will be more than happy to assist if you kindly ask.

» The Sea of Diamonds: The name says all that needs to truly be said about this location. The Sea of Diamonds or Breiðamerkursandur as it is sometimes referred to as is the most photogenic place you will ever see. It is often the place that many TikTok travel accounts have dedicated their time to showcasing as this wondrous landmark is surprisingly not as visited as some of Iceland's other spectacular spots. You may be asking yourself the question, why is Breiðamerkursandur called the Sea of Diamonds? That is because this black sand beach is home to over 1000 pieces of large and bulky icebergs that are scattered throughout the glimmering beach. These pieces come from the Breiðamerkursandur glacier and have slowly begun to break apart, landing themselves on the sand due to the strong current of the icy waters. The shadowy dark sand combined with the bright watery icebergs is a beautiful sight to see that everyone should take the time to visit.

» Breiðamerkurjökull: Forming from the nearby glacier, Breiðamerkurjökull is truly breathtaking to see. As the glacier breaks and the ice around it melts, a gorgeous site is created and forms into the centuries-old lake. What makes this site popular to see is the way in which the light reflects it during the sunset and sunrise. Depending on the day that you visit, the colors coming off of the water can either be made of pinks and oranges or blues and greens. During the winter, the Breiðamerkurjökull form ice caves that can be walked into and through as the newly formed glacier ice connects with the old.

» Puffins: The cutest animals in all of Iceland are the one and only Puffins! Iceland is home to over 8 million puffins that like to make the island their own little oasis. Heimaey and Westman Island are the best part of Iceland to see these fluffy creatures that like to make friends with the local humans. Puffins are an important part of what makes Iceland so much fun to visit. These penguin-like animals enjoy walking with strangers and aren't afraid to take some food right out of their hands. It is perhaps the cutest thing that you can ever see if you are lucky enough to come across one puffin or sometimes even a family of puffins. If this lovely event does occur, just be sure to remember that although puffins are incredibly friendly, they are still wild animals that enjoy their freedom and personal space. Remember to let the puffins come to you, not the other way around.

The Northern Lights

• • • • • • • • • • •

The Northern Lights, otherwise referred to as the aurora borealis, is a series of a colorful and vivid array of lights that occur in the night sky in the Northern hemisphere of the world. They appear in a variety of different shapes and display color patterns that break through the sky on cold nights.

Iceland receives visitors from all over the world every year as on-lookers hope for the one-in-a-million chance to see one of the most incredible events: the Northern Lights. The aurora borealis are visible in Iceland from September through March or mid-April. The chances of having a clear night to experience this are more likely in Iceland as its spot near the Arctic Circle makes it a reliable place to journey to.

Seeing the Northern Lights in Iceland requires some planning in advance. Specifically, it is important to pick the exact area you will want to see them. Here is a list of the top places to see the lights.

» Jökulsárlón: Known by the locals as being the "Crown Jewel of Iceland," the Jökulsárlón glacier is the number one spot in all of Iceland to see the Northern Lights appear in all their glory. It is the place that *feels* the most like a traditional Icelandic view of the extremely beautiful lights. As icebergs break away from the Breiðamerkurjökull glacier, spectacular scenery emerges from Iceland's deepest lake. A boating tour that takes individuals and groups out on the lake gives access to the surreal vision that is this location and allows for the experience to be an intimate event that is secured only for the boat group. The most important reason as to why this stands to be the best place to see the lights is the way in which the surreal colors reflect the water that is surrounded by the pieces of broken icebergs all throughout the lake. If you can only visit one of these locations, Jökulsárlón is the recommended place to be.

» Kirkjufell: This spot is the most photographed mountain in Iceland. The mountain was used for decades as the main landscape in Iceland for landscapers and people from outside the area trying to find their bearings (this was before the use of phones) but was later found to be the perfect spot for photographers to get a clear view of the Northern Lights. The Church Mountain falls is an outstanding waterfall that is only mere feet away from the designated spot on the mountain for pictures. This waterfall acts as a nice lookout point and full visual of Kirkjufell. Although a stunning natural spot during all of the seasons, especially the spring when it is engulfed in luscious green moss, it is September through March when it truly shines. The surrounding areas of the mountain are completely empty for miles with the only thing visible being the peak of Kirkjufell. During the appearance of the Northern Lights, the light comes in through every direction with the stars in the background. This spot is only a two-hour drive from Reykjavík with many shuttle services operating to the mountain.

- - Game of Thrones fans might recognize Kirkjufell for its scenes in the show.
- » Reykjanes Peninsula: This UNESCO-listed geopark has some of the clearest skies in the country that are the necessary amount of minimal pollution that is needed to get this stunning view. This is the top place to see the lights when other areas seem to be experiencing fog, rain, or any other type of difficult conditions. This is because the Reykjanes has experienced far less of these weather occurrences due to where it is situated near the equator. It is also beneficial that the spot itself is actually a subgroup of a large variety of other places to see the Northern Lights. This allows for some freedom in choosing where to go depending on crowds and accessibility based on where you will be staying. Some of these spots include: The Lava Tunnel, Lake Kleifarvatn, and the Grotta Lighthouse. Each of these are top points for seeing the Northern Lights throughout the season.
- » Vík's Black Sand Beaches: Many people dream of seeing a black sand beach with their own eyes. Luckily for those that are lucky enough to get to visit Iceland or even live in the country, there are no shortages of these types of marvelous beaches. The town of Vík has the best view in Iceland. So much so that locals like to create a guide to the best ones for people visiting from outside the

area. Black sand beaches are the norm in Vík due to the nearby volcanic rocks that have spent years becoming cool and stiffened. Going to these beaches is very easy and accessible in Vík and is a fun day trip to make by spending the day exploring the scenery.

Why you should see the Northern Lights in Iceland:

» The main reason? It's Iceland—duh. It is a dream-filled country with white snowy hills and picture-perfect green hills. One could think of a hundred reasons to travel to the country, but it is without a doubt the top selling point of the Northern Lights that takes the cake. While Iceland isn't the only place in the world to see this event take place, it is the most spectacular. Due to a combination of being the perfect distance from the earth's magnetic poles and having the best weather for creating a clear view of the sky, the aurora borealis is an enchanting sight in Iceland. Plus, there are tons of spots all across the country to see them take place. There will be no need for hunting down the best seat in the house because the best seat is on nearly every secluded part of the island.

» The Northern Lights are a life-changing experience to witness. It is something that photos and videos cannot replicate and therefore are much more enchanting in person. Seeing the lights in Iceland is a gift as the country is a big destination spot for individuals to see. Iceland has some of the clearer sights for seeing the Northern Lights, and with so many tours and events that involve getting a glimpse of this one-in-a-million experience, you can be sure that Iceland is the best place to book a trip to.

LESS VISITED ATTRACTIONS THAT DESERVE A DAY TRIP

Hidden Gems

Seyoisfjorour: Iceland's most picturesque town of Seyoisfjorour is so tiny it's easy to miss but definitely not worth it to skip. It has been said that this tiny fishing village is one of the most "tagged" destinations in Iceland on Instagram, but if asked about it, it is not likely that anyone would know where you were talking about when you mentioned the name Seyoisfjorour. The town is famous for its legendary Blue Church that is surrounded by a colorful rainbow striped pathway and a large mountain in the background. This small town is full of Icelandic culture, outdoor activities that include swimming in the lake and serene hiking, as well as outdoor summer concerts that take place right outside the Blue Church. For getting to the town, you won't have to worry about being bored as the drive is undeniably beautiful with magnificent views of the mountains, streams, and other small towns leading to Seyoisfjorour. This spot is good for a day trip or a weekend getaway.

Seljavallalaug Pool: If you are looking for something that is a little bit outside of the basic Iceland itinerary, then the Seljavallalaug Pool may be the day trip you need. The oldest swimming pool in Iceland, the pool was made by an Icelandic man in the 1920's whose goal was to teach people how to swim with the spectacular view of the mountains behind them. This "hidden gem" is used by many as an alternative to the much more populated Blue Lagoon. However, if you don't mind a short hike through stunning landscapes, then the Seljavallalaug is no trouble to get to. The hike itself is only two miles long and is easily walkable and simple to follow. This spot used to be a place that only the locals knew about and frequently visited for a sense of nature and relaxation. It has since gained a small following of tourists that wish to gain the area more popularity. This is an amazing place to get away from the crowds of tourists, but it is important to try to preserve this historical site by not overrunning it with large groups of people and remember to keep as clean as possible—that starts with taking any and all trash with you when you leave. Seljavallalaug Pool tries to keep its space as green as it can.

<u>The Golden Circle:</u> The Golden Circle has a lot to live up to as being one of the major sites to visit when traveling to Iceland. Partly because of the popularity of the Blue Lagoon and the fact that many visitors of the country like to stay within the city center and not travel too far into the more rural areas of Iceland. What so many fail to realize is that the Golden Circle is actually only about fifteen minutes away from the major hotels in Reykjavík—making it a great spot to see for a day trip.

<u>Tvísöngur Sound Sculpture:</u> This odd-shaped sound sculpture comes from the very tiny town of Seyðisfjörður on the opposite end of Reykjavík. These gray-colored and dome-shaped circular structures have been described by many as being "mushroom" looking. They certainly stand out among the vast fields of the mountain on which they sit. Each "mushroom" is connected to one another but what makes them interesting is that each one is a different size, creating an eye-catching look. With a small cut-out door on each dome, there is easy access to the inside that allows for the sound made inside it to travel. The "mushrooms" were created in order to mimic the sound

and tone of the "Icelandic musical tradition of five-tone harmony." It is a unique spin on both art and music with the cultural influence of Iceland's history.

<u>Sky Lagoon:</u> Often mistaken by its similar name to the Blue Lagoon, the Sky Lagoon gets its name from the spectacular view and the description of "where the ocean meets the sky." Its purpose has always been to promote health and wellness through a relaxation ritual in the steaming geothermal spa. This more modern lagoon opened in 2021 and offers fewer crowds and a view of the ocean, making it a great alternative to its counterpart. You might even get to see the Northern Lights at the Sky Lagoon based on its geographical location!

If You Only Have One Week: (Sites, Camping, Hiking, Northern Lights)

● ● ● ● ● ● ● ● ● ● ● ● ●

Day 1 Arrive in the capital city of Reykjavík. Take in the scenery with an evening walk through the city. Walking is the best way to see the beauty of Reykjavík as it is a fairly compacted city with tons to do and see. For the first day, start by checking out Iglesia Hallgrímskirkja, the largest church in the country that reaches 244 feet.

Next, head to some of the well-known neighborhoods to discover the many colorful buildings and houses that Reykjavík has to offer.

Of course, a day in Reykjavík is not complete without seeing the infamous Sun Voyager sculpture created by artist Jón Gunnar Árnason. The sculpture has become a symbol of hope, freedom, and progress since its unveiling in 1990. It stands to represent Iceland as a whole and is most notably recognized for its beauty against an Icelandic sunset.

After an eventful day, you can rest assured that there are plenty of food options to find a good meal and an amazing view to sit back, relax and watch the sunset.

Side Note: Iceland is an expensive country for many visitors to travel to. As a tip to save money during this 7-day camping itinerary, stop off at a local grocery/market store to get food. While not all of your meals need to be cooked at home (or outside while camping), it can be a nice treat to avoid spending too much on restaurants and street food.

Day 2 After getting introduced to Iceland and its wonders, get up early for a day at sea. Iceland earns extra points for having some of the most incredible wildlife that is viewable by tours and other group events. There are numerous boat companies throughout Iceland that begin in the city of Reykjavík and take you all over neighboring towns and ports to see the animals of Iceland. These tours typically last between 4–6 hours. Many tours will end in the town of Grindavík—the home of the Blue Lagoon.

As your tour day comes to an end, soak up the late afternoon in the steaming warm waters of the Blue Lagoon spa. This spa is unlike anything else in the world and is a place that people travel from all over to experience. Arriving later in the day is the best option for avoiding too many people.

While seeing this wonder is not possible without at least a small crowd of people, fewer groups tend to arrive after 4 p.m.

Day 3–6 It's time to go camping! While the idea of camping is not for everyone, Iceland is quite possibly the best place in the world to swap out a hotel bed for a tent and sleeping bag.

Camping is an easy endeavor due to the easy road access and the number of tours given to travelers. It is also a cheap alternative to a nearly unavoidable expensive accommodation.

The first stop of the camping trip begins at Hvolsvöllur Valley. After completing camp setup, it is time for a tour of the Golden Circle. The great thing about the campsite is its closeness to the site. The Golden Circle is one of many natural wonders of Iceland that is a must-see for first-time visitors to the country.

Following this stop at a natural wonder, it is time to make way to the famous black sand beach. Besides being a unique site of actual black sand, it is then that you will travel to another famous Icelandic site. It is the chance in a lifetime to witness the abandoned plane that sits on the beach just near the water's edge at Sólheimasandur.

Your next day or two can be spent going on a food tour, hiking to waterfalls, relaxing at a hot spring, or doing just about any outdoor activity that your imagination could create.

Day 7 After a week of exploring glaciers, hiking through water streams, walking past luscious greenery, and swimming in hot springs, it is time to say farewell to Iceland. Although you will be packing your bags and saying goodbye to this uniquely inhabited land, the memories made will last you a lifetime. As a treat, have a final traditional breakfast meal of hafragrautur and cod liver oil—fit for a Viking!

Where to Eat in Iceland

Iceland is known for many things. It is their food cuisine that perfectly embodies the culture and history of the country, making traveling to Iceland an exciting trip to make. These are some of the best places to get a bite to eat throughout the cities and towns of Iceland. These range from budget-friendly quick stops to 5-star restaurants.

- » **Sjávargrillið: Located in Reykjavík**
  - This famous seafood restaurant in Reykjavík has indoor and outdoor dining options as well as take-out and delivery that makes it a convenient place to get a bite to eat. Good and quality food that is served in an excellent presentation as well as A+ service makes for a fabulous experience. This restaurant has an average rating of 4.5/5 stars in

categories such as *healthy food in Reykjavík* and *Steakhouse and Seafood*.

- Menu Recommendations: White Chocolate Cake, Humar Salat (Sushi), Skelfisk Pasta

» **101 Reykjavík Street Food: Located in Reykjavík**

- A top-rated street food vendor that caters to all food lovers. This traditional noodle-based dish restaurant is the go-to place for trying some Icelandic dishes in the form of seafood and meat meals. Their lobster soup and classic Fish and Chips is the most popular dish to order at 101 Reykjavík Street Food and is recommended to all that decide to try it out. This restaurant is affordable, tasty, and all ingredients including meat and seafood is produced and caught sustainably and ethically. Rated a solid five stars by visitors and ranked as the number four place to eat in all of Reykjavík, you can be sure you're getting the best food that Iceland has to offer.

- Menu Recommendations: Icelandic Skyr Strawberry Cake, Icelandic Traditional Lamb Meat Soup, Vegetable Noodle Soup

» **Café Loki: Located in Reykjavík**

- Serving only traditional Icelandic food and desserts while being located in a picturesque setting of the beloved Hallgrímskirkja church is Café Loki (also known as Kaffi Loki). Their classic dishes include thin rye bread served with butter and/or jam, a unique rye bread ice cream, and steamed cod served warm. The menu for Café Loki is the true selling point as they have a variety of delicious plates to offer. This is a family-run business that aims to bring a "heartwarming traditional" experience to your Iceland adventure. The guest book speaks for itself on this one. With hundreds of honest and loving reviews and drawings being displayed right as you walk through the door.

- Menu Recommendations: Icelandic Plate Loki, Icelandic Plate Freyja, Carrot Cake with Cream

» **Lamb Street Food: Located in Reykjavík**
    - Book a table or order takeaway at Reykjavík's own Lamb Street Food. This restaurant has one goal of preserving Iceland's culture and traditions through the use of food while also maintaining a healthy influence of other nationalities' cuisine choices. The result of this unique endeavor is savory foods that are perfect for breakfast, lunch, and dinner. All food is made and produced to be environmentally friendly, plastic free, organic, and as least wasteful as possible. A nutritional value example list is

available to all customers in order to fully understand each of the ingredients used to source and make the menu items. For large groups of friends or families getting together, Lamb Street Food has the incredible Party platters that feature some of their favorite items being sourced in one take-out packaging.

- Menu Recommendations: Black sheep, Haystack, Kofta (a must try), Cream Cheese and choc

» **Rub 23: Located in Akureyri**
  - Iceland's many seafood restaurants add to some friendly competition between restaurant owners. Rub 23 takes its ranking of being the number two restaurant in all of Akureyri very seriously with an appetizing menu of fish, sushi dishes, and desserts. Everyone that leaves this restaurant can attest to the cozy atmosphere and friendly service that they experience during their dining. With freshly caught fish, fruit, and meats served daily, Rub 23 has a menu full of variety that allows for everyone to get something they are craving.
  - Menu Recommendations: Thai braised beef short ribs, Sushi plate, Rainbow roll, Sticky tofu pudding

- **The Grill House (Grillmarkadurinn): Located in Reykjavík**
    - Iceland's special cuisine is a delicious and unique palette of ingredients that should not be missed. However, even when traveling to a new country it can be nice to try a variety of foods and desserts. The Grill House is the perfect place for getting a large selection of different types of food options. It is a sort of melting pot of services that include whale shark meat, lamb, duck, Greek, and other European dishes. The restaurant itself is made in a cozy atmosphere and caters to large groups.
    - Menu Recommendations: Butcher Steak, Homemade Ice Cream Bliss, Burrata Cheese
- **Hofnin: Located in Reykjavík**
    - Like so many hardworking restaurants in Iceland, this one is family owned and run. Unlike other local food places, this one has been around since the 1930s and has remained a highlight for Icelandic seafood since its opening. It is at Hofnin that you can find the most gorgeous view of the area while being seated on a terrace overlooking the wharf. Specializing in seafood, there is so much to choose from on their lunch, dinner, and happy hour menu.

- Menu Recommendations: Shellfish soup, Broich Torrija ice cream, Gull beer

» **Cafe Babalu: Located in Reykjavík**
- Known for their world-famous cheesecake and friendly service, Cafe Babalu is hard to miss. With its bright orange-colored building and colorful blue door, you know you can start your day at Iceland's most cheerful cafe. You can also be sure you're getting a good view of the location as the Hallgrímskirkja church is directly across the street.
- Menu Recommendations: Caramel Apple crepe, Vegan chili, Swiss Mokka

» **Floran Garden Bistro: Located in Reykjavík**
- This garden cafe is a place to go to find a quiet space that gives guests the perfect Zen experience. This space is designed with a lovely lily pad stream and small walkable bridge that you can appreciate while having breakfast, lunch, or dinner.
- Menu Recommendations: The Garden Soup of the Day, Rice pudding, Slow cooked lamb shank

» **Sandholt: Located in Reykjavík**
- A bakery that is right in the center of all of Reykjavík's action. Serving organic coffee, pastries, lunch, and breakfast, this is a down-to-earth place to chill out and spend some time in before embarking on a day in the city.

- Menu Recommendations: Caprese samloka, Vaffla með ávöxtum, rjóma og hlynsírópi, Sveppa Samloka

Interesting & Traditional Foods

● • ● • ● • ● • ● • ● • ● • ●

» Icelandic Fish: The people of Iceland love some good locally caught fish. There are tons of different variations of cooking methods and exact fish types to choose from when ordering an Icelandic Fish Dish. The Atlantic cod is the go-to order for most first-time visitors to the area. This is because cod plays a major role in the ecosystem of Icelandic waters. The dish provides protein, healthy fats, and most importantly—there will forever be enough cod for people to enjoy and fishermen to catch.

» Fermented Shark: More commonly referred to by its traditional name of Hákarl, this food is a one-of-a-kind type dish. It is made from a type of sleeper shark, most often a Greenland shark, and is a staple in Icelandic food. The shark is prepared by first beginning the fermentation process and then hanging the shark up for a total of five months. It can sometimes be called the rotten shark dish due to the strong odor that leaves it during its hanging process. The end of the journey to creating a fermented shark is to dry it and create a type of "hard" fish texture. It can be served in a number of different ways after it is at the end stage of drying and presenting. This dish was originally the perfect meal for Vikings who ate it on a regular basis for its nutrient value. Now, the fermented shark is considered to be a delicacy in Iceland and is used as a callback to a unique part of history.

» Skyr: Quite possibly the most easily recognizable food item from Iceland is skyr. This is because skyr dates all the way back to the age of the Vikings during the early 800 A.D. when they first settled in Iceland. For a large portion of the world, skyr is not an everyday item that would be at your local food market. But while you may not have directly heard of the name before, more than likely, you have tried an example of skyr in your life. So—what is skyr? It is simply soured milk cheese that consists of a thick texture that is packed with healthy proteins that is completely fat-free. When looking at this product and/or tasting it as someone that has never visited Iceland, your first thought may be that this is a type of yogurt that has a far more sour side to it than sweet as yogurts commonly have. However, the people of Iceland do not categorize this product as being yogurt. It is instead located in the aisle of cheese, as skyr is just a form of cheese that has been made into a more creamy texture. What is interesting about skyr is how much it has become ingrained in the Icelandic food culture. In fact, a large part of most people from Iceland's diet is based on eating skyr every day in some form or another. The popular way to eat this dish is for breakfast with overnight oats or for dinner on the side with a main dish. The process of making skyr has remained primarily the same for centuries: heat up milk, old batches of skyr, and mix. Today, the product is made the same in Iceland but has changed in the United States and other countries in the way in which the milk distribution is produced. This is why the flavor, texture, and overall taste changes depending on where you are trying skyr.

» Cheese and Ice Cream Dish: Cheese and ice cream probably isn't the first thing that comes to mind when searching for the best dessert to have but for the people of Iceland, this treat is actually very popular. The combination of the sweet ice cream and somewhat sour flavor of the cheese makes for a delicious tangy dish. Iceland is full of tiny shops to stop off at and try this cheese and ice cream treat. These shops tend to be run by homemade and locally produced products that add a unique flare to them.

» Icelandic Pancakes: We've all heard of Belgium waffles but what about Icelandic pancakes? This food item is actually more of a crepe than a traditional pancake that many of us tend to picture. But the fluffy pancake and sticky syrup you might be thinking of are not what the people of Iceland like their morning breakfast to be. More often than not, these crepe-like pancakes are served with a light serving size of whipped cream and a side of jam and stay in a very thin texture. It is a tasty treat to start the day off with as a breakfast with a warm tea on the side. If you want to get a bit fancier with your ordering of an Icelandic pancake, you can certainly try adding some fruit, yogurt, and/or honey to the pancakes for some extra protein and flavors.

» Rye Bread: Known throughout Iceland as Rúgbrauð, rye bread is the main source of bread products in the country. Rye bread first gained popularity in Iceland because of its versatility in ways in which it can be used to make a tasty meal and also due to the low cost of the grains. This is one of the most hearty breads that you can eat and for Icelanders, rye bread is made to be put on all sorts of delicious foods. It is most often found to be made in very thin slices that can be served traditionally either smoked or cured. The bread is often mistaken for being dry and/or not filled with flavor, but Rúgbrauð is incredibly sweet and packed full of sugar which makes it a popular choice for combining it with salty snacks such as salmon. Rye bread is considered a traditional food source in Iceland and is great for a snack or with a full meal.

» Hot Dogs: Seeing hot dogs on a list of foods that you need to try when traveling to Iceland is odd. Not because hot dogs are popular but because the obsession that Iceland seems to have on the food is pretty wild. Icelandic hot dogs are not like hot dogs from any other country in the world. In fact, they are very much different due to the way in which they are made and the ingredients put in them. In the majority of countries where hot dogs are popular, the primary meat of choice is pork and beef, sometimes with chicken. Icelandic hot dogs replace these meats with lamb but will add pork or beef to it to add even more zesty flavors. The lamb is 100% organic with the animals being raised in the most environmentally clean and ethical land. On top of that, the many condiments that are used include onions, capers, brown mustard, herbs, and more. These condiments along with the bun are served warm and steamed.

» Licorice: It has been said that Iceland is actually "in love" with licorice due to how much of it is produced and consumed in a year. They have licorice everything including licorice-covered raisins and gummy snacks. This love comes with the fact that over the years, Iceland has created a ban on many nationwide candies. The end result of this ban was that Icelanders still had a sweet tooth that needed to be dealt with in some way or another. Licorice is also an easy commodity to come by with the somewhat strict isolation that comes with imports in the country. Now, a great deal of candy and chocolate is sold through the base marketing of licorice. One of the most popular treats throughout the island is the Lakkris candy bar which includes licorice covered in milk chocolate. If you are visiting Iceland, it is surely worth it to stop off at a local candy store to try some true Icelandic licorice.

» Brennivín: This signature Icelandic drink can be difficult to explain what it actually is. Locals call this drink the "Black Death" as it relates to the jet-black label design and unique flavor that mixes dill and a multitude of spices. The drink can be served as a cocktail or simply as a soda type drink but is above all else a Scandinavian treat that Icelanders have been partaking in since the 1600s.

» Happy Marriage Cake: Iceland's Happy Marriage Cake (Hjónabandssæla) is an easy dessert to make and most definitely a delicious treat. The Marriage Cake is made with the main ingredient of rhubarb along with sugar, crumble, and occasionally jam. After using these three ingredients as the base, it is basically a free-for-all in terms of what else the baker would like to add and how to decorate it. It is also up to the baker to decide how sweet they would like the cake to be, although traditionally, Icelandic Happy Marriage Cake is tart and buttery. This is a dessert that can be found easily throughout the country and is great for a summer night in Iceland.

Icelandic Culture: What You Need to Know

• • • • • • • • • • • • •

Iceland is the number one country in the world for sustainable living and being an environmentally friendly nation. It is the goal of the people to achieve a cut of 55% of all greenhouse gasses by the year 2030. Iceland has nearly reached an average of 100% renewable energy as of 2022.

There are 30 active volcanoes in Iceland that see frequent eruptions that are generally unpredictable. These volcanoes tend to be harmless but do often evoke fear in those that are unfamiliar with their occurrences. Tourists are likely the first to shout "help" when they see these eruptions as they are not used to the pattern of these active mountains. It is for these reasons that the term "Tourist Eruptions" has been used to describe these events.

Iceland is an expensive country for tourists during all seasons. Food prices, entry into parks, and accommodations are all marked high due to Iceland's steep VAT (or Tax) percentage of roughly 24%. The country has remained the third most expensive country in the world to visit. It is possible to travel to and discover Iceland on a budget. However, it is important to prepare for high costs.

The average climate in Iceland is cold, windy, and rainy. This is because of its close proximity to the North Pole and high latitude. It makes for harsh weather conditions and minimal warmth. (The warmest recorded day in Iceland's history came in 1939 with a temperature of 89 degrees Fahrenheit.)

The people of Iceland are proud and strong and love to showcase their beautiful nation. Literature, art, books, and music are just some of the areas in which Iceland wins as having a diverse culture. Visitors of the country should take advantage of the first-class museums, art exhibits, music festivals, and shows that take place throughout the year in Iceland.

Unique Holidays & Events

● ● ● ● ● ● ● ● ● ● ● ● ● ●

» <u>Thorri:</u> The holiday of Thorri has an interesting history that comes from Norse mythology. It is a mid-year celebration that was first recorded in the 18th century and involved festivals, feasts, and poetry that was used to honor the frost month. Today, it is a custom that involves families and friends getting together to have a large and lively meal with traditional foods, songs, and celebrations for Iceland's independence. Many cooks look back at the Viking age for inspiration on what to cook for a specific day. This can include different meat and fish-based meals such as lamb, ram, fermented shark, and liver. All of which the Icelanders' Viking ancestors indulge themselves in. This holiday occurs between the end of January to the beginning of February.

- » <u>Bóndadagur (Husband's Day) & Konudagur (Wife's Day)</u>: Most of us are familiar with Mother's Day and Father's Day, but it is not often that a holiday specifically for spouses is talked about. Iceland celebrates both of these national holidays on the first and last day of Thorri.
- » <u>Summer Solstice:</u> June 21st is the longest day out of the year in Iceland. It is during this day that people get out of their homes to celebrate this fun day during the summer. During this long day, the sun never quite disappears and instead casts a view unlike any other in the world of bright orange and red light throughout. This national holiday often features fun parades, carnivals, and other festivals that are best attended in Reykjavík.
- » <u>Independence Day:</u> Iceland's Independence Day occurs on the 17th of July in honor of Jón Sigurðsson's birthday, a man who fought vigorously to win Iceland its independence. Independence Day is a day full of celebrations, festivals, parties, and get-togethers between family and friends. In the capital city of Reykjavík, a 'Lady of the Mountain' is picked to be the national symbol for the country during that Independence Day. After the woman is chosen, a day of dancing and entertainment takes place in the city center with the 'Lady of the Mountain' leading these events. It is also during Independence Day that top musicals are often

called to perform and offer fun for the whole community.

» <u>Christmas & Christmas Eve:</u> The holiday of Christmas is the most celebrated in the world, but Iceland likes to take it to the next level with festivals, activities, and parades as well as long-standing traditions when it comes to their celebration. For one, Christmas in Iceland is not a one-day event. Instead, it occurs for a total of twenty-six days. It is one of the ways that Christmas in Iceland is so unique and unlike any other country or culture. An almost full day of Christmas is sure to get you into the holiday spirit.

Besides there being thirteen Santa Claus figures, there are also what is known as the Yule Cat or "jólakötturinn." This figure is both mysterious and mischievous and is a symbol for "misbehaving" kids during the season. Since this figure is known for hating Christmas and anyone celebrating it, parents use the story to encourage children to be on their best behavior and avoid encouraging the Yule Cat.

It isn't uncommon to see Christmas trees hanging from a ceiling, wall, or door. While this tradition seemingly has no real explanation, it is something fun that Iceland partakes in that differs from other regions around the world. However, given the lack of all types of trees in the country, do not be shocked if and/or when you see a different type of Christmas tree being displayed. This could be in the form of wood, lights display, or even a tree made of cloth.

Christmas gifts are opened by most families as a celebration after their dinner meal on Christmas Eve. It is when everyone gets together in a relaxed setting and embraces the holiday.

» <u>Verslunarmannahelgi:</u> This national holiday otherwise known as Mud-Football or Party Weekend is a unique event that takes place over the course of three days in the month of August (think Rush week at college). This is Iceland's largest festival and contributes to the majority of the country's domestic flight routes with people flying into Reykjavík for festivals and parades. While anyone is welcome to celebrate this holiday, it is mainly used by young people to get together and form a type of music festival filled with friends, parties, and dancing. There are round-the-clock parties and campsite setups all throughout the city that come in handy for budget-style travelers who want to have a good time hanging out with the locals. If wishing to attend this event, be sure to check for the types of parades and concerts you want to see as there are often multiple to choose from during the party weekend.

<u>Ban on beer:</u> Beer in Iceland has always had an interesting history to it. Like many other countries and

nations, Iceland evoked a ban on alcohol during the early twentieth century. However, when this ban was eventually disbanded, the law remained sealed on beer until the 1980s. Since the beverage was deemed illegal for several decades, the drink never found as large popularity as other neighboring countries had. Instead of beer, the people of Iceland found and continue to find different ways to explore their alcoholic creativity. There are now many tours of local breweries that have a passion for beer drinks and beer-like substances to taste and vote on a favorite.

> » <u>Babies are left outside and alone:</u> This tradition may seem out of the ordinary to many cultures and citizens of countries outside of Iceland but for Icelanders, this is standard practice. For generations, the custom of leaving infants outside, particularly in the snow, has played a role in the way in which children are raised. But this is no case of neglect or intention of harm. In fact, many researchers suggest this is actually beneficial to babies in a number of ways. For one, infants tend to sleep better while taking naps outside as they are able to inhale fresh air and promote healthy lung function at a young age.

This curious custom may raise the question, "Well, is it safe?" Given Iceland's history of being one of, if not the most, safe country to raise children in, it is not often the worry of parents that a child is in an unsafe situation.

Similar to other Icelandic traditions, this one arose from the Vikings but became popular in the 1920s when parents were looking for ways to get their children away from unsafe housing ventilation systems. They believe clean air to be a better alternative.

Visa Information

Countries apart from the EU as well as others such as the United States are not required to apply for any form of visa so long as their stay does not exceed 90 days. The official Iceland website holds more information along with a list of countries that *do* require a visa. https://www.visiticeland.com/article/passport-and-visa-regulations

A digital nomad visa is available to anyone working remotely that is wanting to stay in Iceland on a long-term basis. The average length of stay of this form of visa is 180 days. It also allows digital nomad workers to bring family members along with them such as children and/or other dependents, spouses, and parents.

TOURS & CRUISES

• • • • • • • • • • • • •

Iceland has incredible and in-depth tours for all ages and capabilities. Whether you want your tour to focus on history and information or nature and relaxation, there is a perfect tour for everyone that ensures all visitors get the chance to see as much of the country as possible.

Landmannalaugar Tour: Known as a geothermal wonderland of lava fields, mountains, hiking paths, and striking landscapes, this location brings in visitors at an amicable rate. It is a place rated one of the best to bathe in natural waters. You won't regret booking a tour to travel to this off-the-beaten-track destination. However, picking the tour that works best for your schedule and itinerary can be challenging since many Landmannalaugar tours include add-ons that feature guides to places outside the area. *Arctic Adventures* does a variety of different tours with different options that provide the best experience to its guests. The Landmannalaugar Safari Super Jeep Tour is a crazy fun day filled with adrenaline-rushing jeep traveling, blue waterfalls, and swimming holes to participate in. If you are looking to spend more time exploring Landmannalaugar, then the 3-Day Landmannalaugar Pearl of the Highlands has everything in store for a perfect itinerary. This tour includes hiking, swimming, and nearby town tours.

Game of Thrones Tour: *There are multiple Game of Thrones tours to choose from. The "Gray Line" tour is a recommendation.* Any and all fans of the fantasy series should jump at the opportunity to see the real-life sites from scenes of Game of Thrones. This tour introduces you to the paths that characters such as Sansa and Arya Stark walked, the filming location of the "Wall," and a tour guide who, unlike Jon Snow, knows *everything* about Iceland and its top spots to see. This nine-hour day requires some hiking and long walks, so anyone wishing to take the tour should remember to bring comfortable shoes and clothing. The best part of taking the "Gray Line" tour is getting to see the places in which the actors filmed some of the most memorable scenes in the entire show!

Katla Ice Cave (Under the Volcano) Tour: Checking out caves in the Southern parts of Iceland is a dream come true with the Katla Ice Cave tour. The fourth largest glacier cave in Iceland is available for tours all year round. This tour is just a forty to forty-five-minute drive by jeep from the town of Vík. The drive itself is worth taking this tour for even if ice caves aren't your thing. This is because during the drive to the destination, views of black sand terrain, waterfalls, and mountains are all visible. Once at the cave, astonishing sites await.

Multi Countries Cruises (Iceland): While technically speaking Iceland does not have a close "neighboring" country, it does in fact have a close distance to many other European destinations. Taking a cruise takes away the hassle of trying to handle multiple itineraries, accommodations, and transportation between countries. Prices and dates differ based on which countries you are wishing to sail through from Iceland:

- » Iceland & Ireland (12 nights) $2250
  https://www.celebritycruises.com/itinerary-details
- » Iceland & Greenland (12 nights) $9444
  https://www.celebritycruises.com/itinerary-details/
- » Iceland & Norway (13 nights) $8–10,000
  https://www.globaljourneys.com/trip/viking-cruises-vkiml-r

Holland America Line (Iceland): One of Holland America's favorite cruises is the Iceland line that takes its guests in a full circle lap around the country. Cruises by Holland America are jam packed with tons to do and see. Because of the amount of activities and sights that await, these cruises are between 14–41 days! With so many days to explore the country, Holland America takes its guests outside of Iceland and through other European nations that are "neighbors" to the country of "Fire and Ice." The most popular cruise is part of the Viking series and takes guests through the same route that the true Vikings took when they were making their way to this newfoundland. These cruises give easy access to some of the most well-known places in Iceland, making it a perfect destination trip for all ages of people. Taking a Holland America cruise works best for travelers that are wanting to see as much of the country as they can while also getting to visit nearby countries such as the Netherlands, Italy, Great Britain, Denmark, and more.

- **Popular Cruises:**
    - 14-Day Northern Isles $2479: Circle through Iceland
    - 25-Day Canada, New England & Iceland $5009: From Reykjavík to Akureyri
    - 20-Day Viking Passage $3749: Iceland to Rotterdam

Best of Iceland (Whale-Watching Tour): There are more tours and cruises in Iceland than most people would probably know what to do with. This can lead to some overwhelming moments of trying to come to a decision on which cruise or tour is the best option for you and/or the people you are traveling with. Whale-watching tours are especially popular in Iceland because of the many whale species that frequently make an appearance in the Icelandic waters. Iceland's unique geography makes for a special habitat for these whales (specifically orca whales). A plus to whale-watching tours is that they are available for nearly half of the year. Whales generally come into the Reykjavík area around early spring and will stay till the end of July or beginning of August. However, these dates do not guarantee that you will encounter the ocean's giants. The Icelandic town of Ólafsvík is the best chance of being certain that you will spot at least one species of whale. The town is the starting point for most of the whale tours as the Snæfellsjökull Glacier works as a meeting point for pods of both orcas and the sperm whales. Male sperm whales have been known to lurk in these waters for far longer than most would expect. Although it is not completely understood why these whales enjoy the Snæfellsjökull Glacier so much, it is an oddity that male sperm whales have been spotted in deep waters as early as fall. If you're lucky enough to be in this small town at the exact right time, then there is an even bigger chance at getting a close look at some whale species that aren't normally as often spotted by on-lookers. These include minke whales, humpback whales and even the white-beaked dolphin. Tours are your best chance at getting a look at the world's largest mammals and are easily accessible to nearly all travelers. Here are some of the top whale-watching tours in Iceland:

- » LakiTours https://lakitours.com/
- » Elding Whale Watching https://elding.is/
- » Whale Watching & Dolphin Luxury Yacht Cruise https://www.tripadvisor.com/AttractionProductReview-g189970-d19604165-Whale_Watching_Dolphin_Luxury_Yacht_Cruise-Reykjavík_Capital_Region.html

Getting Around

• • • • • • • • • • • • •

Arriving at either the Keflavík International Airport or the Reykjavík Domestic Airport, you may find yourself a bit overwhelmed with how to possibly get started on your journey through Iceland. Luckily, the country is fully equipped with all sorts of ways to help their tourists see most of the country as easily as possible.

- » <u>Renting a car:</u> If possible, renting a car is by far the best way to see the country with the freedom of not having to rely on a guide or other transportation system. There are many locations in the country that are difficult to reach without the use of a car. It is also a good idea if you are someone that is looking to create a specific itinerary or want to be able to visit places that are not as popular in the tourism industry. Iceland has tons of car rental services for both short-term and long-term uses to make the most out of your trip.

- Best Car Services in Iceland:
  - Cars Iceland
  - Blue Car Rental
  - Hertz

» <u>Bus system:</u> Iceland's two major cities are the best places to rely on the public transportation system. These are known as the Strætó buses. It is important to note that this bus service does not allow for a hop on and off the system and instead means that some planning in advance is necessary. What makes this a good way to travel is that it is cost-efficient and travels to almost every major and popular spot in the country.

» <u>Tour/shuttle company:</u> Going through some sort of tour guide or shuttle is a great experience because it promises a strict routine of seeing all of the most important sites and attractions. It is also a good way of keeping to a budget and not having to worry about driving on difficult terrain as Iceland has a number of roads and pathways that can be challenging for an inexperienced driver to attempt. Shuttle buses are comfortable in Iceland and have routes that begin at most major hotels in the Reykjavík area. Tours are another option for getting around the country. They allow for a more distinct itinerary that doesn't come with a shuttle service. These are more likely to be less cost-efficient but far cheaper than a car rental.

- » <u>Walking</u>: Getting around on foot may seem like a daunting experience to have to go through in order to travel from one area to the next but it is fairly easy—especially if in the capital city of Reykjavík. Because of its small size compared to other major European cities, it is actually recommended by many Icelanders to walk in order to see all of the popular sites. Some of Iceland's smaller towns and cities are also created in a way that makes them accessible to visitors that don't have a means of a car rental or shuttle service.

Honorable Mentions
(Iceland Destinations & Things to Do)

Chocolate Cooking Lesson: Halldór Kristján Sigurðsson is known throughout Iceland as being the teacher to tourists that wish to learn the ways in which chocolate is made and consumed in Iceland. His most popular classes are in Reykjavík in a small food truck that he has made into the perfect classroom. The lessons taught go deep into the world of chocolate and the impact that it has on the Icelander as the dessert is not known for being the most purchased good. However, according to Halldór, tourists love the chance to learn something new and appreciate the delicious treat in a way that others sometimes forget to do. Halldór uses a combination of different molds to form unique and fun designs on his chocolate. These include little lambs and imprints of cocoa beans.

Outside of Halldór's fun lesson there are other chocolate lessons to embark on in Iceland. "Creative Iceland" is a chocolate factory in Reykjavík that gives tours of their factory to guests and lets them learn the process of making what they claim to be "the very best chocolate you could have."

Cave Hiking: Iceland's hiking is incredible, but for the experts who may want to "up the ante" on their adventurous hikes, a cave hike can certainly be the way to achieve this. Cave hikes occur during the winter months and are usually only available with a tour and guide. These guides take you through multiple ice glaciers, some of which are world known as being incredibly stunning and naturally made. Cave hikes are thrilling and a sure-fire way to get your heart pumping as each step gets you deeper into the frozen world. Tours and guides last for one to two days and range in cost from $100 USD to $400 USD on average.

Wildlife Tour: A wildlife tour is an obvious choice for a day of activities when traveling to Iceland. The country has made a name for itself in the way in which it handles environmental issues along with sustainability and health, making it a naturally thriving place for wildlife to reside in. Wildlife tours are not hard to come by, so picking when to go means you can plan to see exactly the animals you have always been interested in seeing in their natural habitat. These tours can center around animals of all sorts, but some of the best include a trip out to sea for a whale-watching tour, where orcas frequently make an appearance. Of course, no tour is complete without at least one sighting of a puffin and their little family. Puffins are easy to spot and are very friendly towards humans. One might even attempt to jump on the tour with you.

(During the right season, you can combine a wildlife tour with the Northern Lights.)

Hofn Town: Visiting the town of Hofn is a fun way to get away from the busy scene of Reykjavík and other nearby areas where people tend to flock to. Hofn is a fishing village with just over two-thousand people as its population. It is situated off of Iceland's South Coast region and is the place in which Iceland's largest glacier can be found. This settlement is the capital town for getting the best seafood, especially lobster and has many locally caught fish markets situated throughout the town.

Grimsey Island: The holy grail for fishing and all things seafood is Grimsey Island. This tiny and barely inhabited island is home to only one-hundred residents. What it lacks in a human population, it makes up for in seagulls. This tiny island is a popular spot for spotting wildlife that lurk in the cold waters. Things include different species of both birds and whales as the primary animals. In the year 1222, Grimsey Island was first mentioned in modern records as being the place of settlement for a Viking battle that is sadly to have been thought to have been ruthless. Nevertheless, the island has since become a symbol for peace and is one of the reasons why wildlife are respected and valued so fiercely. This island can be visited through a tour during all seasons. It is especially unique to visit during the cold winter months because of the ocean waters becoming frozen and thus creating walkable icebergs.

Interesting Facts

- » Swimming between the two continents of North America and Europe is possible in Iceland and is the only place in the world that allows for this unique tectonic plate connection.
- » While most of the world knows just one Kris Kringle, Iceland has as many as thirteen Santa Clauses. They are referred to as Yule Lads.
- » With a population of less than 350,000, Iceland has only two cities that hold at least 10,000 citizens.
- » Elves, trolls, and creatures are important parts of Icelandic culture as tales of these mythical beings date back to the Viking Ages. Many people today believe that these beings are still around and living among them.
- » Iceland was ranked the number one country in the world for safety in the year 2022 and has remained on the list of safe places to visit since 2009.

- » Last names in Iceland differ based entirely on a combination of a child's mother and father's first names.
- » There are 200 waterfalls scattered throughout the country of Iceland.
- » Though most would assume a nature-filled country such as Iceland would be home to many insects, the country does not have any mosquitoes for a reason that is still unknown to scientists.
- » Reading is an essential part of living in Iceland. 1 out of every 10 people has published their own book, and the most popular gift is to give and receive books.
- » A letter in the mail does not require an exact address or name. Instead, people will often draw maps to show where they wish the letter to arrive.
- » Fast food is difficult to come by. Unlike countries such as the United States or the United Kingdom, Iceland does not make it a habit to encourage these sorts of cuisines. Starbucks, McDonald's, and 7-Elevens have all been closed in the last two decades.

The country of Iceland is in and of itself a natural wonder of the world. With sky-towering waterfalls, blue-colored streams, and hikes that take your breath away, it is no wonder that Iceland receives over 700 thousand outside visitors every year.

Anyone searching for a trip full of adventure and beauty should look no further than the land of "Fire and Ice."

References

Iceland Population, World Meter
   https://www.worldometers.info/world-population/iceland-population/

Quick Facts, The Big Picture
   https://www.iceland.is/the-big-picture/quick-facts/

What Language Is Spoken in Iceland? Babbel Magazine
   https://www.babbel.com/en/magazine/what-language-is-spoken-in-iceland

Best Time to Visit Iceland – Pros and Cons of Each Season https://icelandwithaview.com/best-time-visit-iceland-case-seasons/

The Climates and Seasons of Iceland
   https://www.lotuscarrental.is/blog/the-climates-and-seasons-of-iceland

Currency & Money
   https://www.icelandontheweb.com/articles-on-iceland/travel-info/currency-money/

Iceland by electric bike: Why you should absolutely try renting an e-bike the next chance you get
https://electrek.co/2022/06/05/renting-an-e-bike-in-Reykjavík-iceland/

A History of Reykjavík
https://guidetoiceland.is/Reykjavík-guide/a-history-of-Reykjavík

Reykjavík national capital, Iceland
https://www.britannica.com/place/Reykjavík

A Short History of Reykjavík
https://Reykjavíkcityguide.is/a-short-history-of-Reykjavík/

Seasons and Climate

https://www.lotuscarrental.is/blog/the-climates-and-seasons-of-iceland

https://icelandwithaview.com/best-time-visit-iceland-case-seasons/

https://www.frommers.com/destinations/iceland/planning-a-trip/when-to-go

Accommodations

Loft - HI Hostel & Bar
https://www.hostel.is/Reykjavík

The Retreat at Blue Lagoon Iceland
https://www.bluelagoon.com/accommodation/retreat-hotel

Eric the Red Guesthouse
https://sites.google.com/view/eric-the-red-guesthouse/

Reykjavík Domes http://www.Reykjavíkdomes.com/

Hallgrímskirkja church https://visitReykjavík.is/service/hallgrimskirkja-church

Lava Hostel https://lavahostel.is/

Design Cottage Close to Icelandic Countryside & Reykjavík https://www.airbnb.co.uk/rooms/plus/18736637?adults=1&children=0&infants=0&check_in=2023-03-27&check_out=2023-04-03&federated_search_id=1011d5d2-60a9-4914-ae18-5d25e3716fde&source_impression_id=p3_1660660717_EQtztbdjYmhxbi0L

Hotel Viking https://www.hotelviking.com/?utm_source=google-gbp&utm_medium=organic&utm_campaign=gbp

Adorable 1-bedroom guesthouse in Hafnarfjörður https://www.airbnb.co.uk/rooms/578056205602364614?adults=1&children=0&infants=0&check_in=2023-02-05&check_out=2023-02-12&federated_search_id=1011d5d2-60a9-4914-ae18-5d25e3716fde&source_impression_id=p3_1660660762_ABb0c%2FHWgvjLAC5N

Thríhnúkagígur Volcano: Inside the Volcano https://insidethevolcano.com/

Húsavík Cape Hotel https://www.Húsavíkhotel.com/

Fosshotel Húsavík https://www.islandshotel.is/hotels-in-iceland/fosshotel-Húsavík

Árból Guesthouse https://arbol.is/

Húsavík Green Hostel https://www.Húsavíkgreenhostel.is/

Óbót 1. — riverside cabin https://www.airbnb.com/rooms/

Downtown Egilsstaðir Apartment 1 https://www.airbnb.com/rooms/43567531?source_impression_id=p3_1662187721_t30CaRw6f%2FkLzgy4

Adorable little guesthouse with private bathroom https://www.airbnb.com/rooms/5544249?

Beautiful Cottage at Kaldá Lyngholt https://www.airbnb.com/

Lovely 1-bedroom apartment close to Black Beach https://www.airbnb.com/rooms

Hótel Vík https://www.stayinvik.is/

Hótel Kría https://www.hotelkria.is/

Black Beach Suites https://www.airbnb.com/rooms/

Hótel Ísland Comfort https://uk.hotels.com/ho274182/hotel-smari-Kópavogur-iceland/

201 Hotel https://uk.hotels.com/ho657707840/201-hotel-Kópavogur-iceland/

A city hotel by the lake https://uk.hotels.com/ho443167/hotel-kriunes-a-city-hotel-by-the-lake-Kópavogur-iceland/

Hótel Heiðmörk
> https://uk.hotels.com/ho655550368/hotel-hei-mork-Kópavogur-iceland/

Iceland & Ireland
> https://www.celebritycruises.com/itinerary-details

Iceland & Greenland
> https://www.celebritycruises.com/itinerary-details/

Iceland & Norway
> https://www.globaljourneys.com/trip/viking-cruises-vkiml-r

Facts

https://www.trafalgar.com/real-word/facts-about-iceland/

https://www.britannica.com/place/Iceland

https://adventures.is/information/iceland-facts/

Verslunarmannahelgi
> https://grapevine.is/travel/practical-information/2011/07/29/verslunarmannahelgi/

https://mountaineers.is/verslunarmannahelgi/

The Unique History of Beer in Iceland
> https://www.icelandtravel.is/blog/cuisine/the-history-of-beer-in-iceland/

Babies https://www.oattravel.com/community/the-inside-scoop/travel-trivia/baby-its-cold-outside?icid=isc-ymal_2_img

https://www.scarymommy.com/scandinavian-babies-nap-outside-cold-weather

https://guidetoiceland.is/connect-with-locals/nanna/icelands-independence-day

https://www.icelandtravel.is/blog/june-in-iceland/

https://www.icelandair.com/blog/midnight-sun-in-iceland/

https://sonianicolson.com/blog/husbands-day-bondadagur

https://www.icelandreview.com/news/today-is-womans-day/

https://www.icelandicroots.com/post/2013/01/24/traditions-and-history-of-thorri

https://www.icelandair.com/blog/thorri-and-goa-history/

Tours

Welcome to Iceland Tours
https://www.icelandtours.is/

Multi-Day Tours in Iceland
https://adventures.is/iceland/multiday-tours/

Whale Watching Trips https://www.adventure-life.com/iceland/tours/whale-watching

Elding Adventure https://elding.is/

Trip Advisor
https://www.tripadvisor.com/Attractions-g189952-Activities-c61-t188-Iceland.html

Laki Tours https://lakitours.com/

https://icelandmonitor.mbl.is/news/news/2017/08/17/teaches_tourists_to_make_icelandic_chocolate/

Icelandic chocolate making Factory tour and Tasting https://creativeiceland.is/culture-and-food-icelandic-chocolate-making-factory-tour-and-tasting-Reykjavík-iceland

Whale Watching & Dolphin Luxury Yacht Cruise https://www.tripadvisor.com/AttractionProductReview-g189970-d19604165-Whale_Watching_Dolphin_Luxury_Yacht_Cruise-Reykjavík_Capital_Region.html

The Game of Thrones Tour https://grayline.is/tours/Reykjavík/game-of-thrones-tour-8706_88

Cave Tour https://adventures.is/iceland/day-tours/ice-caves/katla-ice-cave-tour-under-the-volcano/

https://guidetoiceland.is/connect-with-locals/regina/the-spectacular-katla-ice-cave-in-south-iceland-is-open-all-year-round

Landmannalaugar tour https://adventures.is/iceland/day-tours/landmannalaugar/

Visa Information https://www.visiticeland.com/article/passport-and-visa-regulations

Transportation

https://www.visiticeland.com/article/public-transport

Car Rentals https://www.kayak.com/Iceland-Car-Rentals.111.crc.html

https://www.enterprise.com/en/car-rental/locations/iceland.html

https://www.bluecarrental.is/

Renting a Car in Iceland: 14 Essential Tips https://www.twowanderingsoles.com/blog/ultimate-guide-to-renting-a-car-in-iceland

Food

https://outside-oslo.com/icelandic-happy-marriage-cake-hjonabandssaela/

https://www.foodlustpeoplelove.com/2021/06/icelandic-happy-marriage-cake.html

https://roamingtaste.com/hjonabandssaela-icelandic-happy-marriage-cake/

https://www.deliciousmagazine.co.uk/recipes/happy-marriage-cake/

https://icelandmag.is/article/what-exactly-brennivin

https://www.atlasobscura.com/articles/iceland-licorice

https://www.kingarthurbaking.com/recipes/icelandic-rye-bread-rugbraud-recipe

Sandholt https://sandholt.is/en/getting-started/

Floran Garden Bistro http://www.floran.is/floranenglish

Cafe Babalu https://www.babalu.is/

Hofnin https://hofnin.is/en/

The Grill House (Grillmarkadurinn)
https://www.tripadvisor.com/Restaurant_Review-g189970-d2371613-Reviews-Grillmarkadurinn-Reykjavík_Capital_Region.html

https://www.grillmarkadurinn.is/en

Rub 23 https://www.rub23.is/

Lamb Street Food https://www.lambstreetfood.is/en

Café Loki https://loki.is/

101 Reykjavík Street Food
https://www.tripadvisor.com/Restaurant_Review-g189970-d16720175-Reviews-101_Reykjavík_Street_Food-Reykjavík_Capital_Region.html

https://101Reykjavíkstreetfood.is/

Sjávargrillið
https://www.tripadvisor.com/Restaurant_Review-g189970-d2145648-Reviews-Sjavargrillid_Seafood_Grill-Reykjavík_Capital_Region.html

Activities

Tvísöngur Sound Sculpture
https://visitseydisfjordur.com/culture/tvisongur-soundsculpture/

https://guidetoiceland.is/connect-with-locals/regina/the-sound-sculpture-tvisongur-in-seydisfjordur

The Golden Circle https://guidetoiceland.is/best-of-iceland/top-9-detours-on-the-golden-circle

https://www.findingtheuniverse.com/iceland-golden-circle/

https://expertvagabond.com/golden-circle-iceland/

Seljavallalaug Pool https://icelandtrippers.com/seljavallalaug-pool-iceland/

https://www.eyvindarholt.is/places-to-visit/seljavallalaug-geothermal-pool/

Seyoisfjorour https://visitseydisfjordur.com/

https://www.laidbacktrip.com/posts/seydisfjordur-iceland-travel-guide

Vík: https://guidetoiceland.is/travel-iceland/drive/reynisfjara

https://www.thediscoveriesof.com/reynisfjara-black-sand-beach-iceland/

https://adventures.com/iceland/attractions/cities-towns/vik/

http://www.szirine.com/blog/2004/07/05/village-life-in-vik-iceland/

https://guidetoiceland.is/travel-iceland/drive/vik-i-myrdal

https://guidetoiceland.is/connect-with-travel-bloggers/eat-sleep-love-travel/5-top-things-to-do-in-vik

https://www.tripadvisor.com/Attractions-g189978-Activities-Vik_South_Region.html

Reykjanes Peninsula https://www.visitreykjanes.is/en

Breiðamerkurjökull https://guidetoiceland.is/travel-iceland/drive/breidamerkurjokull

https://troll.is/breidamerkurjokull-the-glacier-of-the-crystal-blue-ice-caves/

Puffins https://adventures.is/blog/puffins-in-iceland/

https://www.icelandtravel.is/blog/inspiration/8-best-spots-to-spot-puffins-in-iceland/

https://grayline.is/blog/puffins-in-iceland

https://wonderfulwanderings.com/best-place-to-see-puffins-in-iceland/

The Sea of Diamonds https://www.nordicvisitor.com/blog/diamond-beach-attraction-guide-iceland/

Blue Lagoon https://www.bluelagoon.com/

https://www.travelandleisure.com/trip-ideas/nature-travel/iceland-blue-lagoon-vs-sky-lagoon-which-to-visit

https://guidetoiceland.is/best-of-iceland/blue-lagoon-the-ultimate-guide

Reykjanes Lighthouse https://www.visitreykjanes.is/en/place/reykjanes-lighthouse

1973 US Navy C-117D Sólheimasandur Crash https://amazingiceland.is/destination/the-story-of-dc3-or-c-117-plan-wreck-on-solheimasandur/

Kópavogur

https://guidetoiceland.is/travel-
iceland/drive/Kópavogur

https://www.Kópavogur.is/en

https://visitReykjavík.is/city-areas/Kópavogur

Things To Do
https://www.tripadvisor.com/Attractions-
g1093088-Activities-
Kópavogur_Capital_Region.html

https://www.expedia.com/Things-To-Do-In-
Kópavogur.d6084321.Travel-Guide-Activities

Egilsstaðir

https://www.tripadvisor.com/Attractions-g315847-
Activities-Egilsstaðir_East_Region.html

https://visitEgilsstaðir.is/en/things-to-see/11-top-
things-to-see-around-Egilsstaðir/

https://www.icelandtravel.is/attractions/Egilsstaðir/

https://www.odysseytraveller.com/articles/Egilsstaðir-
iceland/

https://www.east.is/en/service/east-iceland-heritage-
museum

https://www.travelocity.com/Things-To-Do-In-
Egilsstaðir.d1110.Travel-Guide-Activities

Húsavík

https://www.northiceland.is/en/destinations/towns/Húsavík

https://guidetoiceland.is/travel-iceland/drive/Húsavík

https://www.getyourguide.com/Húsavík-l87259/Húsavík-original-whale-watching-t85302/

https://www.tripadvisor.com/Attractions-g189963-Activities-Húsavík_Northeast_Region.html

https://traveo.is/what-to-see-and-do-in-Húsavík/

Culture House
    https://www.sagatrail.is/en/museums/Húsavík-culture-house/

https://www.lonelyplanet.com/iceland/the-north/Húsavík/attractions/culture-house/a/poi-sig/1377011/359570

https://www.roughguides.com/iceland/myvatn-and-the-northeast/Húsavík/

Hafnarfjörður

https://visitReykjavík.is/city-areas/Hafnarfjörður

https://adventures.com/iceland/attractions/cities-towns/Hafnarfjörður/

https://hiticeland.com/towns_and_villages_in_iceland/hafnarfj%C3%B6r%C3%B0ur

https://visitReykjavík.is/event/Hafnarfjörður-christmas-village

https://icelandmonitor.mbl.is/news/culture_and_living/2020/11/30/christmas_village_opens_in_Hafnarfjörður/

https://www.viator.com/Reykjavík-attractions/Hafnarfjörður/overview/d905-a15308

https://guidetoiceland.is/travel-iceland/drive/Hafnarfjörður

Reykjavík

https://www.britannica.com/place/Reykjavík

https://www.icelandtravel.is/attractions/Reykjavík-2-2/

https://guidetoiceland.is/Reykjavík-guide/a-history-of-Reykjavík

https://Reykjavíkcityguide.is/a-short-history-of-Reykjavík/

https://electrek.co/2022/06/05/renting-an-e-bike-in-Reykjavík-iceland/

https://www.eater.com/maps/best-restaurants-Reykjavík-iceland

https://www.lonelyplanet.com/iceland/Reykjavík

https://www.forbes.com/sites/davidnikel/2022/05/01/10-fascinating-facts-about-Reykjavík-iceland/

Walking and Trekking Iceland, Paddy Dillion.